P9-DVV-243

BISON BOOKS

Letters of a Civil War Nurse
Cornelia Hancock, 1863–1865

EDITED BY

Henrietta Stratton Jaquette

Introduction to the Bison Books Edition by
Jean V. Berlin

UNIVERSITY OF NEBRASKA PRESS
LINCOLN AND LONDON

Introduction © 1998 by the University of Nebraska Press
All rights reserved
Manufactured in the United States of America

⊗ The paper in this book meets the minimum requirements of American
National Standard for Information Sciences—Permanence of Paper for
Printed Library Materials, ANSI Z39.48-1984.

First Bison Books printing: 1998
Most recent printing indicated by the last digit below:
10   9   8   7   6   5   4   3   2   1

Library of Congress Cataloging-in-Publication Data
Hancock, Cornelia, 1840–1927.
[South after Gettysburg]
Letters of a Civil War nurse: Cornelia Hancock, 1863–1865 / edited by
Henrietta Stratton Jaquette; introduction to the Bison books edition by Jean
V. Berlin.
p. cm.
"Reprinted from the 1971 edition, titled South after Gettysburg: letters of
Cornelia Hancock from the Army of the Potomac, 1863–1865, by Books for
Libraries Press, Freeport, N.Y."—T.p. verso.
ISBN 0-8032-7312-6 (pbk.: alk. paper)
1. Hancock, Cornelia, 1840–1927—Correspondence. 2. Nurses—United
States—Correspondence. 3. United States—History—Civil War, 1861–
1865—Medical care. 4. United States—History—Civil War, 1861–1865—
Personal narratives. 5. United States—History—Civil War, 1861–1865—
Women. I. Jaquette, Henrietta Stratton, b. 1881. II. Title.
E621.H29   1998
973.7'75—dc21
98-10011   CIP

Reprinted from the 1971 edition, titled *South After Gettysburg: Letters of
Cornelia Hancock from the Army of the Potomac 1863–1865*, by Books for
Libraries Press, Freeport NY.

To
ISABEL P. CHILD

INTRODUCTION
Jean V. Berlin

Cornelia Otis Hancock was a remarkable woman. The letters contained in this volume give us a glimpse of only a few years of her life, when she served as a nurse with the Union Army. But all of her adult life was spent in helping others—though nursing, teaching, and reform. Her devotion to bettering the lives of all Americans, regardless of race and class, was absolute, and her belief that education would elevate the lives of children unwavering.

She was born on February 8, 1840, at Hancock's Bridge, a small community outside of Salem, New Jersey. Both her parents were Quakers whose families had come to New Jersey before the Revolution, and several of her ancestors had been active in politics. This religious and political heritage, combined with a reasonably large family fortune, equipped her well for work in philanthropy. But her family lived a quiet life in a small town, and her opportunities for work were few. Her sister Ellen had managed to get a job at the U. S. Mint in Philadelphia and later married a Quaker doctor, Henry T. Child, who ministered to the wounded during the war. The Quaker Hancocks felt strongly that the Civil War was a just war, their abolitionist beliefs outweighing their propensities for nonviolence. Hancock's only brother enlisted in the Union service, as did several of her cousins, in 1862. She herself yearned to be of service to her nation, and she got her chance after the Battle of Gettysburg. Her brother-in-law knew of her desire and asked her to come to the town as a volunteer nurse to help with the wounded in the aftermath of the fighting. In an oft-quoted incident, Dorothea Dix turned down her services, "on the score of my youth and rosy cheeks" (p. 3). Dix, it was well known, objected to attractive, unattached nurses on the grounds that they and the men would be too interested in romance. Not easily swayed, Hancock went ahead and got on the train, leaving Child to argue with Dix about whether she would go to Gettysburg. Hancock would see nursing service of one kind or another for virtually the rest of the war, with a small break spent at the Washington DC home for "Contraband," blacks who had fled servitude for what they thought would be the safety of federal lines. It is from her letters home during these years that this volume is adapted.

This book is what could be called a second-generation memoir of the war and Reconstruction. Though Hancock wrote these letters at the time, they were not published until 1937. Hancock herself was long dead, as were nearly all of the major actors described. Consequently, there was less need for censorship, although Ms. Jaquette, Hancock's relative and literary executor, had instructions of some kind, as witnessed by her destruction of a bundle of letters labeled "to be burned without reading" (p. xx). Nonetheless, the question of authorial agenda is not as significant as in other accounts, as Hancock herself made no overt attempt to shape her letters into a narrative. Because of this, the lessons they do impart are all the more striking.

Like most other young women both North and South who worked as nurses during the war, Hancock found her duties limited by conventional expectations to reading to the soldiers, writing letters for them, helping them to eat, and providing general comfort. But her duties quickly escalated as both the needs and numbers of patients rose. Once they had proven to authorities that they could be of real, medical use, nurses still found themselves battling prejudices on the homefront, as Hancock's letters show. Repeatedly, she reassured her family that she was not living a scandalous life, that camp living was not riotous and lascivious, that soldiers did not wander into her cabin at all hours of day and night seeking to "defile" her. "The Salem people have got up a perfect panic about the 'way' I live. I wish they could know the exact state of things, they would calm their fears," she wrote (p. 78). "I cannot explain, but there is so much distinction in different rank, and I rank about as high as anything around. No soldier would be allowed to come into my house without knocking even in the day time and at night they could not get in without sawing out the logs," she rejoined to the repeated notion that she was in physical danger (p. 80). "There is no danger from any thing in the army, except an *unsophisticated* individual might possibly have their affections trifled with," she concluded (p. 80). What comes through in her narrative is her belief that she was at last living the life she had wanted. She became depressed, worried, and frustrated from time to time, but she never seriously voiced a wish to return home. The work she did and the friends she made allowed her to feel that her life was full. Like many other women, Hancock found that the war provided her with opportunities to escape the restrictions of class and gender. But unlike many other women, Hancock continued to search for and find these opportunities after the guns stopped firing.

War itself disturbed and sickened her: although she became used to the sights, sounds, and smells of the wounded, she still believed that "the idea of making a *business* of *maiming men* is not one worthy of a civilized nation" (p. 69). She was horrified to find that the lack of organized, disciplined health services added to the number of casualties, and that many of those who wished to be seen as angels of mercy were actually more concerned with their own rank and perquisites than the needs of the wounded. She threw herself into getting what the men needed regardless of regulations and found that her reputation for selflessness and efficiency helped her to get more done; the authorities assumed that when she came to them with a request it was not frivolous and deserved a hearing (pp. 53, 117). The shipments she received from various Quaker aid societies were quickly and efficiently distributed, and she kept an iron control over her supplies. There were few medical personnel who did more for their patients than she did. One Christian Commission agent wrote, "One can but feebly portray the ministrations of such a person. She belonged to no association—had no compensation. She commanded respect, for she was lady-like and well educated; so quiet and undemonstrative, that her presence was hardly noticed, except by the smiling faces of the wounded as she passed."[1]

Hancock's letters also give us an invaluable look at life behind the lines in the famous Second Corps. In spite of the bloody fighting, much of army life was lived in camps, particularly during the winter months, and Hancock gives her readers some of the flavor of that life, albeit at a more refined level than that experienced by many of the common soldiers. In particular, her accounts of the shifting friendships and alliances among the medical personnel reveal an intense world where relationships were quickly formed and trying experiences created strong bonds. These are experiences common among all levels of army life, and it is instructive to see how women were welcomed into this world and generally well treated by men who appreciated both their sacrifices and their ability to bring a little of the vanished world of peacetime into the camps.

ix

At the end of the war she returned to her sister and brother-in-law's house in Philadelphia, where time hung heavy on her hands. She eagerly accepted an offer from the Friends' Association for the Aid and Elevation of the Freedmen to go south with educator Laura Towne and start a school for black children near Charleston. She had long been interested in the plight of the newly freed blacks, commenting as early as December 1863, during her time at the Contraband Hospital, that "you could not help thinking where are all those good abolitionists north that do so much *talking* and so little *acting*" (p. 35). She arrived in South Carolina in January 1866 and quickly and accurately assessed the state of affairs for blacks: "Take from the negro the protection of such men as Gen. Saxton and the good men of the Freedman's Bureau and you will have inaugurated as near an approach to slavery as it is possible."[2] Her letters from 1866–68, though not included in this edition, were published by the Thomas Y. Crowell Company in 1956. These later letters paint a poignant portrait of a time of great possibilities, of African American adults and children eager to learn, knowing that true citizenship and equality began with education, but finding innumerable obstacles in their way. Ultimately, they would be denied this education by the ignorance and apathy of the Northern public and the prejudices and hatred of Southern whites. This was a moment of great opportunity, one that the nation squandered.[3] Hancock would remain at her post for nearly ten years, resigning in 1875 for reasons of ill health.

Hancock's career in reform continued after her return north. As outlined in Henrietta Jaquette's introduction to these letters, she worked for the Society for Organizing Charity in Philadelphia's Sixth Ward, inaugurating a number of programs that, with their emphasis on education, children, and teaching women the principles of household management, bring to mind the activities of Jane Addams at Hull House in Chicago. Addams, also a Quaker, had been inspired by the same reform movements in London as had Hancock, who had visited London during her time in Charleston. Hancock would help to found the Children's Aid Society of Pennsylvania in 1882 and remain on the board of the charity until 1895. Her interest in helping the poor to help themselves through information and education took a different turn in the late 1880s when she became involved with the slum community of "Wrightsville" in south Philadelphia. Her friend Edith Wright had leased the dilapidated houses from their absentee owners and was determined to create an experimental community that would demonstrate how the poor could end the cycle of poverty with the correct encouragement and advice. Wright asked Hancock to be her on-site agent, and she enthusiastically accepted, earning the residents' trust and helping them to upgrade their houses and create a community infrastructure. The ultimate success of the project came in 1914, when the last tenants were able to buy their houses. Now seventy-four, Hancock retired to Atlantic City, New Jersey, where she lived with a niece until her death thirteen years later.

Unlike more prominent reformers such as Hull, Hancock did not publicize her work, which accounts for her relative obscurity until the publication of her letters. Rather than write about her work, she got on with it. She never married and had no regrets about it, wryly commenting to her mother in 1866 that "Men, as the generality of them appear in public life, have few charms for me, and if thee has any lingering hopes of my yet in my advancing years committing matrimony, thee must keep thy anticipations in good check for the Freedmens Bureau or Secessia will not be likely to send to thee a valuable son-in-law."[4] Her tenderness for the surgeon Frederick Dudley died quickly after the war. She had earlier voiced misgivings about his treatment of his hired black servant, and a falling-out between them over postwar politics and Reconstruction seemed inevitable. She had known he was no abolitionist, but a unionist, and she would have found his attitudes hard to swallow in light of what she knew about the conditions of the freedmen. She found contentment and fulfillment in her activities and a family in those she had helped. When she died, she left behind a substantial legacy in the lives she had enlightened and the schools she had created. Her editor wrote her epitaph best: "She felt she could be of use; though she did not know of the many ways which would open to her later—during the War; after it in the South among the Negroes; and later in Philadelphia among the poor and neglected of a great city" (p. xviii).

xi

NOTES

1. L. P. Brockett, and Mary C. Vaughan, *Women at War: A Record of Their Patriotic Contributions, Heroism, Toils and Sacrifice during the Civil War* (1867; rpt., Stamford CT: Longmeadow Press, 1993), 286.

2. Henrietta Stratton, Jaquette, ed., *South after Gettysburg: Letters of Cornelia Hancock 1863–1868* (New York: Thomas Y. Crowell, 1956), 195.

3. Those interested in another account of working with the freedmen should consult Gerald Schwartz, ed., *A Woman Doctor's Civil War: Esther Hill Hawks' Diary* (Columbia: University of South Carolina Press, 1984, 1989). Dr. Hawks makes an appearance in Hancock's diary, and vice versa.

4. *South After Gettysburg* (1956), 249.

CONTENTS

✿

ILLUSTRATIONS

✿

FOREWORD

✿

"The Florence Nightingale of America," Captain Charles Dod called Cornelia Hancock as he wrote to his mother of the ministering care he received when taken seriously ill during the Civil War at City Point Hospital. This was before the days of Red Cross with its roll of enlisted trained nurses ready for war or disaster, with first-aid kits, hospital supplies, and a system that has stood the test of many experiences. In 1863, nurses were volunteers, with ingenuity and pressure of necessity their only teachers. It was as assistant to her sister's husband, Dr. Henry T. Child, of Philadelphia, that Cornelia Hancock reached the battlefield after Gettysburg, and again after the Battle of the Wilderness, but the place she made for herself with the army doctors and with her grateful soldier patients ensured to her, in spite of her youth, continuous service in a Second Corps Hospital until Richmond was taken. These letters—to her mother at home, to her sister in Philadelphia, to her brother, and to young nieces and nephews—cover the two years of her volunteer service as nurse.

Hancock's Bridge, her birthplace, was a remote tiny village four miles beyond Salem, in southern New Jersey. Once it had been the scene of stirring events in Revolutionary days, and a hundred years before that Cornelia's ancestors were pioneer settlers from England, coming to this country just after William Penn. Service as colonial legislators and judges, martyrdom in the Revolutionary War, and a sturdy part in the development of a new nation were in her blood, but in the quiet country life which contented her father, opportunity for her as a woman was confined to teaching in the village school, or marriage. She longed to be in the midst of things herself when her only brother and her cousins went to the War against the South in

1862, and she began canvassing every possible opportunity to follow them. She felt she could be of use; though she did not know of the many ways which would open to her later—during the War; after it in the South among the Negroes; and later in Philadelphia among the poor and neglected of a great city.

When the War was over, she turned eagerly to other fields of usefulness. Her few months' experience among the contraband—escaped Negro slaves—in Washington in the winter of 1863–64 convinced her of the Negroes' need for help and education; so, under the auspices of the Philadelphia Yearly Meeting of the Society of Friends, she went south in 1866 with Laura Towne to help start schools. Their companionship on that journey to South Carolina showed Miss Towne that Cornelia Hancock had initiative and resourcefulness, so she sent her off on her own, and the Laing School was started in Pleasantville, South Carolina, by the courageous young Quakeress from Hancock's Bridge. A pioneer among Negro schools, it still continues its work.

After ten years in South Carolina, Cornelia Hancock came north and went with friends to England. Here she was interested in Great Britain's problem with its growing number of poor. She gained access everywhere and learned how the older city of London met these problems. From the Old World she brought back to Philadelphia ideas about organized and constructive help for the needy, and about housing in the poorer districts of the city. In the home of her brother-in-law, Dr. Henry Child, at 634 Race Street, already well known as a center of humanitarian and advanced ideas, the Society for Organizing Charity was born in 1878—the society now known the country over as the Family Society of Philadelphia. Cornelia Hancock was herself one of the first social workers, as Superintendent having charge of "the poor" in the Sixth Ward. The theory that a worker, giving fully of her time and energies and growing skill in helping people, should serve not only the interests of the people needing help but the desires of those who had means and wanted to help, was a personal philosophy growing from her experience with the Army and in Negro schools of the South. It is the philosophy of modern social work.

Work with the families of the Sixth Ward of Philadelphia convinced her of the need for special aid to children, and so in 1882 with other concerned persons she helped to found the Children's Aid Society and Bureau of Information, now known as the Children's Aid Society of Pennsylvania. She was on the committee which engaged the first paid worker for the new society, and her minutes as secretary of that first Board of Directors reflect her own philosophy:

"We have been anxious not only to do something, but to do it well: to guard the child and to guard society: to help the suffering little one of today, and not, at the same time, to create a pauper for tomorrow. We cannot reconcile it to an enlightened conscientiousness in charity to act without inquiry, blindly trusting that the kind motive will ensure beneficient results."

She was active on this first Board of the Pennsylvania Children's Aid until her resignation in 1895.

Meantime, in 1884, she became the agent and co-worker of Edith Wright in the management of the group of squalid houses known as Wrightsville. Though within Philadelphia City limits, it was well to the south, an isolated village housing many employees of the Philadelphia Gas Works, the Atlantic Refining Company, and of Peter Wright and Company's wheat wharves. The story of this "experiment in the care of property" covers every phase of the modern housing program: philanthropy was balanced by business sense; the same persistence was used with tenants as with municipal authorities, and better ways of living emerged, as Wrightsville grew to know and trust their new "agent," Cornelia Hancock. Again she pioneered: this time in the social advancement of a whole community through "housing," which, as she interpreted it, went beyond sanitation, public utilities and repairs, to improving the school system, providing a library, a savings bank, and recreational opportunities as well. She continued this community work until, by 1914, every tenant became his own landlord. Always her philosophy was to help people help themselves.

Cornelia Hancock died in 1926 at the age of 87. In her later years she talked often to her nieces and younger cousins of her many and varied experiences. It was to me, the granddaughter of a cousin, that she gave her letters written between the years 1863 and 1878. I have not attempted to recount all the activities of her long life; I have desired only to show that the qualities of mind and spirit evidenced by her letters during the years 1863–65 were inherent qualities determining her life work. She saw clearly what needed to be done at the moment and proceeded to do it, or to get it done in the most direct fashion. Results proved that her courage and resourcefulness were founded on intelligence and vision.

She never married. There is room, perhaps, for speculation over a bundle of letters which were left, at her death, "to be burned without reading." Her real interest in Dr. Frederick Dudley with whom she worked in the Hospital at Brandy Station is apparent, as is also his friendship for her. Her anxious concern for his safety at his disappearance after an engagement outside Petersburg in October 1864 is an insistent note in all her letters from October to April when, released from a southern prison, he is again with his regiment.

Her own story of how she "came to go to war" forms the prologue to her letters.

HENRIETTA STRATTON JAQUETTE

I

A YOUNG QUAKERESS
GOES TO WAR

¤

EVEN on a sand-hill one may acquire a reputation for independence of character bordering on eccentricity by doing nothing more than going quietly one's own way and letting one's neighbor go his; and this was the reputation my family had acquired in the little village of Hancock's Bridge, New Jersey, long before the Civil War broke out.

All through the Township, my father was known as "Thomas Y., the fisherman," and as the one man in those parts who was foolish enough to vote for Frémont in the election of 1856. He was a silent man who spent his time thinking and fishing in the little stream known as Alloway's Creek, a tributary of the Delaware, and I never knew of his having any other occupation except that of reading the newspapers. In order to fish more successfully, he went to bed with the tide and got up when it turned; his days and nights were planned solely with reference to slack water. He owned a canoe built to suit himself and to hold but one person. On it were painted the letters "ItyT"—the title having been invented with great care and ingenuity for the exclusive purpose of baffling idle curiosity. No one could pronounce the word or imagine what it meant, and it pleased him never to tell his numerous questioners that the pronunciation consisted in naming each letter separately. We lived on our inherited property and ate fish every day. As it was impossible for us to eat all the fish father caught in Alloway's Creek, a large number was given away to the village people, about six of the finest being reserved

I

daily for our own use. It never occurred to my father to sell them or do anything else to add to the income of the family. We had enough to *live on* and if we wanted more we could get it ourselves—and we generally did.

A nonconformist by nature, my father believed that every man should be a law unto himself. He should carefully avoid interference with the rights of others and take as little interest as possible in other people's affairs. These were the cardinal points of his confession of faith. When I told him one day that I had looked into a neighbor's window as I passed by, and knew exactly what she was putting on her table for supper, he replied that he had walked past that window for fourteen years and had never once looked in, and that I might find something better to do—a reproof I never forgot.

A maternal grandmother, of whom my father used to say: "No teakettle could pour fast enough to suit her without she tipped it over," was supposed to have supplied my brother and myself with ambition enough to overcome the inertia on the other side of the house, and after the War had been a hideous reality for two years and more, it seemed to me that the teakettle of life was pouring out very slowly indeed its scalding stream of anxiety, woe, and endless waiting. After my only brother and every male relative and friend that we possessed had gone to the War, I deliberately came to the conclusion that I, too, would go and serve my country. I confided this resolution to my sister's husband, Dr. Henry T. Child, who lived in Philadelphia where he was well known in philanthropic and antislavery circles. He promised to let me know of the first available opportunity to be of use.

The summons came on the morning of July fifth, 1863, when his horse and carriage was sent for me on a Fourth of July excursion boat that was returning to Salem by the Delaware River. It arrived in the early morning and was driven the five miles beyond the town to where I lived. When it was driven up in front of our house, my mother threw up both of her hands and exclaimed to father: "Oh, Tom, what has happened?" I had not risen, but hear-

2

ing Mother's exclamation, and surmising, I said: "Oh, nothing, Mother. Doctor has sent for me to go to war!" So it proved, and in an hour's time I was off for Philadelphia. I well remember when driving through Salem my friends were going to church, so I hid myself down in the carriage lest I should be stopped to be bidden good-bye or saluted by any of the formalities they might wish to indulge in. Much less did I want to hear them say: "Why, Cornelia, thee is too young to go."

It was late in the afternoon when we reached Philadelphia. The city was wild with excitement over news of a terrible battle which had just been fought on Pennsylvania soil—no one knew exactly where—but it finally became known as having occurred at a little town called Gettysburg. The Rebel army was at first supposed by many to be on its way to Philadelphia. Every hour was bringing tidings of the awful loss of life on both sides. Dr. Child, with a number of other physicians, had determined to leave that night by the eleven o'clock train for Gettysburg. I was to accompany him.

He and the Hon. Judge Kelly had aided Miss Eliza Farnham, a well-known public-spirited woman, with a number of others of "suitable age" to get passes as volunteer nurses. The ladies in the party were many years older than myself, and I was under the especial care of Miss Farnham. At eleven P. M. we were wending our way out Washington Avenue to Broad and Prime streets, then the depot. The darkness, the uncertainty of everything, were appalling, and when we reached Havre de Grace, we heard the cars creaking weirdly on the pontoon bridges over the Susquehanna River. The morning found us in Baltimore where there was stir and some knowledge of events. Here Dorothea Dix appeared on the scene. She looked the nurses over and pronounced them all suitable except me. She immediately objected to my going farther on the score of my youth and rosy cheeks. I was then just twenty-three years of age. In those days it was considered indecorous for angels of mercy to appear otherwise than gray-haired and spectacled. Such a thing as a hospital corps of comely young maiden nurses, possessing grace and

3

good looks, was then unknown. Miss Farnham explained that she was under obligation to my friends who had helped her get proper credentials. The discussion waxed warm and I have no idea what conclusion they came to, for I settled the question myself by getting on the car and staying in my seat until the train pulled out of the city of Baltimore. They had not forcibly taken me from the train, so I got into Gettysburg the night of July sixth—where the need was so great that there was no further cavil about age.

We arrived in the town of Gettysburg on the evening of July sixth, three days after the last day of battle. We were met by Dr. Horner, at whose house we stayed. Every barn, church, and building of any size in Gettysburg had been converted into a temporary hospital. We went the same evening to one of the churches, where I saw for the first time what war meant. Hundreds of desperately wounded men were stretched out on boards laid across the high-backed pews as closely as they could be packed together. The boards were covered with straw. Thus elevated, these poor sufferers' faces, white and drawn with pain, were almost on a level with my own. I seemed to stand breast-high in a sea of anguish.

The townspeople of Gettysburg were in devoted attendance, and there were many from other villages and towns. The wounds of all had been dressed at least once, and some systematic care was already established. Too inexperienced to nurse, I went from one pallet to another with pencil, paper, and stamps in hand, and spent the rest of that night in writing letters from the soldiers to their families and friends. To many mothers, sisters, and wives I penned the last message of those who were soon to become the "beloved dead."

Learning that the wounded of the Third Division of the Second Corps, including the 12th Regiment of New Jersey, were in a Field Hospital about five miles outside of Gettysburg, we determined to go there early the next morning, expecting to find some familiar faces among the regiments of my native state. As we drew near our destination we began to realize that war has other horrors than the sufferings of the wounded or the desolation of the bereft. A sicken-

4

ing, overpowering, awful stench announced the presence of the un-buried dead, on which the July sun was mercilessly shining, and at every step the air grew heavier and fouler, until it seemed to possess a palpable horrible density that could be seen and felt and cut with a knife. Not the presence of the dead bodies themselves, swollen and disfigured as they were, and lying in heaps on every side, was as awful to the spectator as that deadly, nauseating atmosphere which robbed the battlefield of its glory, the survivors of their victory, and the wounded of what little chance of life was left to them.

As we made our way to a little woods in which we were told was the Field Hospital we were seeking, the first sight that met our eyes was a collection of semi-conscious but still living human forms, all of whom had been shot through the head, and were considered hope-less. They were laid there to die and I hoped that they were indeed too near death to have consciousness. Yet many a groan came from them, and their limbs tossed and twitched. The few surgeons who were left in charge of the battlefield after the Union army had started in pursuit of Lee had begun their paralyzing task by sorting the dead from the dying, and the dying from those whose lives might be saved; hence the groups of prostrate, bleeding men laid together ac-cording to their wounds.

There was hardly a tent to be seen. Earth was the only available bed during those first hours after the battle. A long table stood in this woods and around it gathered a number of surgeons and at-tendants. This was the operating table, and for seven days it literally ran blood. A wagon stood near rapidly filling with amputated legs and arms; when wholly filled, this gruesome spectacle withdrew from sight and returned as soon as possible for another load. So appalling was the number of the wounded as yet unsuccored, so helpless seemed the few who were battling against tremendous odds to save life, and so overwhelming was the demand for any kind of aid that could be given quickly, that one's senses were benumbed by the awful responsibility that fell to the living. Action of a kind hitherto unknown and unheard of was needed here and existed here only.

5

From the pallid countenances of the sufferers, their inarticulate cries, and the many evidences of physical exhaustion which were common to all of them, it was swiftly borne in upon us that nourishment was one of the pressing needs of the moment and that here we might be of service. Our party separated quickly, each intent on carrying out her own scheme of usefulness. No one paid the slightest attention to us, unusual as was the presence of half a dozen women on such a field; nor did anyone have time to give us orders or to answer questions. Wagons of bread and provisions were arriving and I helped myself to their stores. I sat down with a loaf in one hand and a jar of jelly in the other: it was not hospital diet but it was food, and a dozen poor fellows lying near me turned their eyes in piteous entreaty, anxiously watching my efforts to arrange a meal. There was not a spoon, knife, fork, or plate to be had that day, and it seemed as if there was no more serious problem under Heaven than the task of dividing that too well-baked loaf into portions that could be swallowed by weak and dying men. I succeeded, however, in breaking it into small pieces, and spreading jelly over each with a stick. A shingle board made an excellent tray, and it was handed from one to another. I had the joy of seeing every morsel swallowed greedily by those whom I had prayed day and night I might be permitted to serve. An hour or so later, in another wagon, I found boxes of condensed milk and bottles of whiskey and brandy. It was an easy task to mix milk punches and to serve them from bottles and tin cans emptied of their former contents. I need not say that every hour brought an improvement in the situation, that trains from the North came pouring into Gettysburg laden with doctors, nurses, hospital supplies, tents, and all kinds of food and utensils: but that *first* day of my arrival, the sixth of July, and the third day after the battle, was a time that taxed the ingenuity and fortitude of the living as sorely as if we had been a party of shipwrecked mariners thrown upon a desert island.

6

II

AFTER THE
BATTLE OF GETTYSBURG

✿

Gettysburg, Pa. July 7th, 1863.

MY DEAR COUSIN

I AM very tired tonight; have been on the field all day—went to the 3rd Division 2nd Army Corps. I suppose there are about five hundred wounded belonging to it. They have one patch of woods devoted to each army corps for a hospital. I being interested in the 2nd, because Will [her brother] had been in it, got into one of its ambulances, and went out at eight this morning and came back at six this evening. There are no words in the English language to express the sufferings I witnessed today. The men lie on the ground; their clothes have been cut off them to dress their wounds; they are half naked, have nothing but hard-tack to eat only as Sanitary Commissions, Christian Associations, and so forth give them. I was the first woman who reached the 2nd Corps after the three days fight at Gettysburg. I was in that Corps all day, not another woman within a half mile. Mrs. Harris was in first division of 2nd Corps. I was introduced to the surgeon of the post, went anywhere through the Corps, and received nothing but the greatest politeness from even the lowest private. You can tell Aunt that there is every opportunity for "secesh" sympathizers to do a good work among the butternuts; we have lots of them here suffering fearfully. To give you some idea of the extent and numbers of the wounds, four surgeons, none of whom were idle fifteen minutes at a time, were busy all day amputating legs and arms. I gave to every man that had a leg or arm off a gill

7

of wine, to every wounded in Third Division, one glass of lemonade, some bread and preserves and tobacco—as much as I am opposed to the latter, for they need it very much, they are so exhausted.

I feel very thankful that this was a successful battle; the spirit of the men is so high that many of the poor fellows said today, "What is an arm or leg to whipping Lee out of Penn." I would get on first rate if they would not ask me to write to their wives; *that* I cannot do without crying, which is not pleasant to either party. I do not mind the sight of blood, have seen limbs taken off and was not sick at all.

It is a very beautiful, rolling country here; under favorable circumstances I should think healthy, but now for five miles around, there is an awful smell of putrefaction. Women are needed here very badly, anyone who is willing to go to field hospitals, but nothing short of an order from Secretary Stanton or General Halleck will let you through the lines. Major General Schenk's order for us was not regarded as anything; if we had not met Miss Dix at Baltimore Depot, we should not have gotten through. It seems a strange taste but I am glad we did. We stay at Doctor Horner's house at night—direct letters care of Dr. Horner, Gettysburg, Pa. If you could mail me a newspaper, it would be a great satisfaction, as we do not get the news here and the soldiers are so anxious to hear; things will be different here in a short time.

CORNELIA

Gettysburg—July 8th, 1863.

MY DEAR SISTER

WE have been two days on the field; go out about eight and come in about six—go in ambulances or army buggies. The surgeons of the Second Corps had one put at our disposal. I feel assured I shall never feel horrified at anything that may happen to me hereafter. There is a great want of surgeons here; there are hundreds of brave fellows, who have not had their wounds dressed since the battle.

8

Brave is not the word; more, more Christian fortitude never was witnessed than they exhibit, always say—"Help my neighbor first he is worse." The Second Corps did the heaviest fighting, and, of course, all who were badly wounded, were in the thickest of the fight, and, therefore, we deal with the very best class of the men—that is the bravest. My name is particularly grateful to them because it is Hancock. General Hancock is very popular with his men. The reason why they suffer more in this battle is because our army is victorious and marching *on* after Lee, leaving the wounded for citizens and a very few surgeons. The citizens are stripped of everything they have, so you must see the exhausting state of affairs. The Second Army Corps alone had two thousand men wounded, this I had from the Surgeon's head quarters. I cannot write more. There is no mail that comes in, we send letters out: I believe the Government has possession of the road. I hope you will write. It would be very pleasant to have letters to read in the evening, for I am so tired I cannot write them. Get the Penn Relief to send clothing here; there are many men without anything but a shirt lying in poor shelter tents, calling on God to take them from this world of suffering; in fact the air is rent with petitions to deliver them from their sufferings.

C. HANCOCK

Direct boxes—E. W. Farnham, care of Dr. Horner, Gettysburg, Penna. for Second Corps Hospital. Do not neglect this; clothing is shockingly needed. We fare pretty well for delicacies sent up by men from Baltimore.

If you direct your letters Miss Hancock, Second Corps, Third Division Hospital, do not scruple to put the Miss to it, and leave out Cornelia, as I am known only by that cognomen. I do not know when I shall go home—it will be according to how long this hospital stays here and whether another battle comes soon. I can go right in an ambulance without being any expense to myself. The Christian Committee support us and when they get tired the Sanitary is on hand. Uncle Sam is very rich, but very slow, and if it was not for the Sanitary, much suffering would ensue. We give the men toast

9

and eggs for breakfast, beef tea at ten o'clock, ham and bread for dinner, and jelly and bread for supper. Dried rusk would be nice if they were only here. Old sheets we would give much for. Bandages are plenty but sheets very scarce. We have plenty of woolen blankets now, in fact the hospital is well supplied, but for about five days after the battle, the men had no blankets nor scarce any shelter.

It took nearly five days for some three hundred surgeons to perform the amputations that occurred here, during which time the rebels lay in a dying condition without their wounds being dressed or scarcely any food. If the rebels did not get severely punished for this battle, then I am no judge. We have but one rebel in our camp now; he says he never fired his gun if he could help it, and, therefore, we treat him first rate. One man died this morning. I fixed him up as nicely as the place will allow; he will be buried this afternoon. We are becoming somewhat civilized here now and the men are cared for well.

On reading the news of the copperhead performance, in a tent where eight men lay with nothing but stumps (they call a leg cut off above the knee a "stump") they said if they held on a little longer they would form a stump brigade and go and fight them. We have some plucky boys in the hospital, but they suffer awfully. One had his leg cut off yesterday, and some of the ladies, newcomers, were up to see him. I told them if they had seen as many as I had they would not go far to see the sight again. I could stand by and see a man's head taken off I believe—you get so used to it here. I should be perfectly contented if I could receive my letters. I have the cooking all on my mind pretty much. I have torn almost all my clothes off of me, and Uncle Sam has given me a new suit. William says I am very popular here as I am such a contrast to some of the office-seeking women who swarm around hospitals. I am black as an Indian and dirty as a pig and as well as I ever was in my life—have a nice bunk and tent about twelve feet square. I have a bed that is made of four crotch sticks and some sticks laid across and pine boughs laid on that with blankets on top. It is equal to any mattress ever made. The tent is open at night and sometimes I have laid in the damp all night long, and got up all right in the morning.

The suffering we get used to and the nurses and doctors, stewards, etc., are very jolly and sometimes we have a good time. It is very pleasant weather now. There is all in getting to do what you *want* to do and I am doing that.

The First Minnesota Regiment bears the first honors here for loss in the late battle. The Colonel was wounded—Lieutenant Colonel, Major, and Adjutant. They had four captains killed outright and when they came out of battle, the command devolved on the First Lieutenant. Three hundred and eighty-four men went into battle, one hundred and eighty were wounded and fifty-four killed. The Colonel I know well; he is a very fine man. He has three bullets in him; has had two taken out by Dr. Child, the other he got in at Antietam and it is there yet. I do hope he will recover. Most of the men are from New York here now; they are very intelligent and talk good politics. McClellan is their man mostly. Meade they think sympathizes with McClellan and therefore they like him. Hooker is at a very low ebb except as they think he fed them well—a circumstance that soldiers make great account of. Such feeders you never saw.

Pads are terribly needed here. Bandages and lint are plenty. I would like to see seven barrels of dried rusk here. I do not know the day of the week or anything else. Business is slackening a little though —order is beginning to reign in the hospital and soon things will be right. One poor fellow is hollowing fearfully now while his wounds are being dressed.

There is no more impropriety in a *young* person being here provided they are sensible than a sexagenarian. Most polite and obliging are all the soldiers to me.

It is a very good place to meet celebrities; they come here from all parts of the United States to see their wounded. Senator Wilson, Mr. Washburn, and one of the Minnesota Senators have been here. I get beef tenderloin for dinner.—Ladies who work are favored but the dress-up palaverers are passed by on the other side. I tell you I have lost my memory almost entirely, but it is gradually returning. Dr. Child has done very good service here. All is well with me; we do not know much war news, but I know I am doing all I can, so I do not concern further. Kill the copperheads. Write everything, however trifling, it is all interest here.

From thy affectionate

C. HANCOCK

2nd Army Corps—3rd Division Hospital
near Gettysburg.
July 21st, 1863.

MY DEAR MOTHER

IT is with trouble that I can find time and quiet enough to write to anyone. I have been sick but one day since I have been here, and then I went into a tent and was waited upon like a princess. I like to be here very much, am perfectly used to the suffering and the work just suits me; it is more superintending than real work, still the work is constant. I like being in the open air, sleep well and eat well. The rumors about camp are that this hospital is to be moved down to Gettysburg. I hope it is not so but I expect it is. The field hospital is a number of tents and nothing more; it is in first rate order now, and I am sorry it has to be moved. All the officers will be changed I suppose. The men are very polite to me and I get on remarkably well, but quiet is impossible to obtain at camp.

I have succeeded in getting a washerwoman today which is a great institution here indeed. Old sheets and pads of every description are wanted in my hospital. Food we are scarce of sometimes but it is generally plenty.

I received, a few days ago, a Silver Medal worth twenty dollars. The inscription on one side is "Miss Cornelia Hancock, presented by the wounded soldiers 3rd Division 2nd Army Corps." On the other side is "Testimonial of regard for ministrations of mercy to the wounded soldiers at Gettysburg, Pa.—July 1863."

SECOND CORPS HOSPITAL

GETTYSBURG

There have been in the Corps Hospital I suppose some thirty women, and it seems I am the favored one in the lot. Several, since they have seen mine, have started a subscription for two other ladies. Most of the ladies are dead heads completely.

The Steward of our Hospital is a funny fellow; he has gone to New York to take some wounded and says he is going to bring me a calico dress. I have no dress now except what is torn in threads. I sent to Belle to make me a new one and send it to me. You need not fear for me, I am all right. From thy daughter—

C. HANCOCK

I get letters from the soldiers that have left here, but do not get many letters from home. I wish you could see the hospital now, but I would never wish anyone to see a battlefield. I have succeeded in getting the men some beef steak for dinner, which I feel very thankful they are to have. The boys are going out on horse-back this afternoon to try to get some butter. I have written probably as much as is practical.

From thy daughter,
C. HANCOCK

[From a Soldier]

Camp Bradford, Baltimore, Md.
July 21st, 1863.

TO OUR SOLDIERS' FRIEND, MISS HANCOCK

YOU will please excuse a Soldier for writing a few lines to you to express our thankfulness for your kindness to our poor wounded comrades after the late battle. You little know the pleasure a Soldier feels in seeing a woman at camp. I only wish that we were able to express our gratitude in a different manner, but "Uncle Sam" happens to be in debt to us and until he "comes down" with his greenbacks we are not able to do any more. You will never be forgotten by us for we often think of your kind acts and remember them with pleas-

13

ure. Please excuse a Soldier for taking the liberty to write to you, for although we are Soldiers we know how to appreciate a kind act.

Your sincere friend,

"A SOLDIER"

3rd Division—2nd Army Corps Hospital—Gettysburg, Pa. July 26th—Sunday.

MY DEAR MOTHER

TODAY is Sunday but there is no semblance of it here. It is now about five o'clock in the morning. Our hospital has been moved and our stores have given out. There is nothing to cook with, hence I have nothing to do, and, therefore, have time to write. Such days will come here that we have to see our wounded men fed with dry bread and poor coffee; and I can tell you it is hard to witness some cursing for food, some praying for it. It seems to be no one's fault but will happen. All the luxuries that the men get come through the Christian Commission, Sanitary, Ladies Aid, etc. I would give anything to have a barrel of butter, and some dried rusk that I have seen in our parlor. I wish you would get up something of the kind and have Mrs. Jones requested to forward to me. I should think it would be as satisfactory for *me* to have them as for them to be sown broadcast on the land. I could make a report of everything I received and write to the Society.

I received a silver medal from the soldiers which cost twenty dollars. I know what thee will say—that the money could have been *better* laid out. It was very complimentary though. One of the soldiers has a sword that he found on the battlefield, which he is going to give to me before I come home. If they were only where they could buy I should be so loaded with baggage, I should never be able to get home. I shall not come home, unless I get sick, while this hospital lasts. I have two men detailed to wait on me, which suits of course. They are now fixing up nice little tables and all such things all around the tent. I have eight wall tents full of amputated men. The tents of the wounded I look right out on—it is a melancholy

14

sight, but you have no idea how soon one gets used to it. Their screams of agony do not make as much impression on me now as the reading of this letter will on you. The most painful task we have to perform here, is entertaining the friends who come from home and see their friends all mangled up. I do hate to see them. Soldiers take everything as it comes, but citizens are not inured. You will think it is a short time for me to get used to things, but it seems to me as if all my past life was a myth, and as if I had been away from home seventeen years. What I do here one would think would kill at home, but I am well and comfortable. When we get up early in the morning, our clothes are so wet that we could wring them. On they go, and by noon they are dry.

From thy affectionate daughter—

C. HANCOCK

General Hospital Gettysburg, Pa.
Aug. 6th, 1863.

MY DEAR SISTER

WE have all our men moved now to General Hospital. I am there, too, but the order in regard to women nurses has not yet been issued, and I do not know what my fate will be; I only know that the boys want me to stay very much, and I have been assigned to ward E. It is a great deal nicer here except that I have but fourteen of my old boys which is very trying—it is just like parting with part of one's family. I go to see the boys and some of them cry that I cannot stay. I have the first four tents abreast of the cook house, the handiest tents in the whole hospital. I have Steward Olmstead for my *headquarter influence*, and we have an elderly doctor for our ward. I have a large hospital tent and sleep with three other ladies, so unless I struggle very hard to find it my friends need fear no harm for me. I am better than I am at home. I feel so good when I wake up in the morning. I received a letter announcing Sallie S's death. It does not appear to me as if one death is anything to me now. I do want my watch very

15

much indeed; if you can get any show of a safe way of sending it—do so; I want my own gold one. I expect I shall be able to draw twelve dollars from the government now, but if thee can draw any money for hospital purposes or for me, send it along, for it is a poor place to be without money. If there should be an opportunity to send my purple dress, best bonnet and mantilla, I should like to have them; this hospital will not stay here more than three weeks and nobody knows what I may want to do by that time. I may come home if there is no other battle. Dr. Dwinelle gave me a splendid recommendation to Dr. Chamberlain, Surgeon in charge here. I am good friends with Sanitary, Christian, and all here, if it only lasts. One of the boys died yesterday, and one had his leg amputated fresh. Cadet Brown I sent to your house to tell you I was well. Col. Colville is getting some better; he expects Dr. Child here.

No citizens are allowed in Camp without a pass only after four o'clock. The militia go around after dark and pick up stragglers to take them out of camp. The other night they asked me if I was a detailed nurse. As it was before I was sworn in, I had to say "No." They said their orders were peremptory, so I would have to go, but Steward Olmstead appeared and told them that I was all right, so they went away. I expect I shall be in the guard house!—but that is only a part of soldiering if I am. I do not meddle or make up with any one here but the ward master, doctor of our ward and Steward Olmstead. We have twenty women here about, some of them are excellent, but a more willful, determined set you never saw. Send this letter to mother for I hate to take the time to write often.

C. HANCOCK

General Hospital—Aug. 8th, 1863.

MY DEAR SALLIE [1]
IT is well that thee is persevering enough to write to me without an answer for it is almost impossible for me to find time to write. In the

[1] Her niece.

morning before breakfast, before the men wake up, is the time we write, for as soon as the men are awake, they want something and continue in that state until late at night. Our hospital is on rising ground, divided off into six avenues, and eighteen tents holding twelve men each on each avenue. We call four tents a ward and name them by a letter; mine is ward E. The water is excellent and there is order about everything. I like it a great deal better than the battlefield, but the battlefield is where one does most good. I shall go to the front if there comes another battle, if not we shall stay in this hospital until fall. If thee was here thee would be very useful to run errands. I make friends with every one on the ground and get on first rate. Sallie S. I hear has passed away. But as surely as I live it does not seem to me as if I should ever make any account of death again. I have seen it disposed of in such a summary manner out here.

It is now about nine o'clock, every tent has a light in it, and a lot of groaning sick men. Our cook-house alone is a sight; they have meals cooked for thirteen hundred men, so you may know that they have to have the pots middling size. If you ever saw anything done on a large scale, it is done so here. There are many sights here, but the most melancholy one is to see the wounded come in in a long train of ambulances after night fall. I must be hardhearted though, for I do not feel these things as strangers do. What is the war news? I do not know the news at all. I never read the papers now, which is a slight change for me. I look at it in this way that I am doing all a woman can do to help the war along, and, therefore, I feel no responsibility. If people take an interest in me because I am a heroine, it is a great mistake for I feel like anything but a heroine.

Miss Dix was in camp today and stuck her head in the tents, but she does not work at all, and her nurses are being superseded very fast. I think we have some excellent nurses; we must have at least thirty women in the whole hospital. I have one tent of Johnnies in my ward, but I am not obliged to give them anything but whiskey.

I have no doubt that most people think I came into the army to

17

get a husband. It is a capital place for that, as there are very many nice men here, and all men are required to give great respect to women. There are many good-looking women here who galavant around in the evening, and have a good time. I do not trouble myself much with the common herd. There is one man who is my right-hand man; he is about nineteen years old—is a hospital steward and will do anything to accommodate.

I want you to direct your boxes General Hospital, Ward E—Gettysburg. Things ought to be sent to Gettysburg, as here is the place where there are the most wounded, whether my name is on them or not. Things are all put into Mrs. Duncan's hands in this hospital; I should not have control as I had at Corps Hospital. I am going to town soon to look after the boxes that have been sent to me.

Thy aunt, CORNELIA

Camp Letterman Hospital—Gettysburg,
Aug. 14th, 1863.

MY DEAR MOTHER

I RECEIVED thy letter this morning and was glad to get it; letters are the desideratum in this part of the world. I am regularly installed in the General Hospital now, and like it better even than the Corps Hospital. The main reason for my staying, aside from duty, is that I am so well, if it only lasts. I feel like a new person, eat onions, potatoes, cucumbers, anything that comes up and walk as straight as a soldier, feel life and vigor which you well know I never felt at home. The place here is very healthy. I cannot explain it, but I feel so erect, and can go steadily from one thing to another from half past six o'clock in the morning until ten o'clock at night, and feel more like work at ten than when I got up at home.

My Twelve dollars per month from the government, if it should come, would pay my washing, and that is all the expense I am at, at present. I got a barrel of pads and dried fruit, and handkerchiefs today from express office. I have not received the box from the Salem ladies yet but I expect I shall.

From thy affectionate daughter—

C. HANCOCK

Camp Letterman, General Hospital,
Aug. 17, 1863.

DEAR MOTHER

I ALWAYS spend my evenings in the post office. I am alive and well, doing duty still in the general hospital. I do think military matters are enough to aggravate a saint. We no sooner get a good physician than an order comes to remove, promote, demote or *something.* Everything seems to be done to aggravate the wounded. They do not get any butter; there is certainly a want of generalship somewhere for there is surely enough butter in the United States to feed these brave wounded. There are many hardships that soldiers have to endure that cannot be explained unless experienced. I have nothing to do in the hospital after dark which is well for me—all the skin is off my toes, marching so much. I am not tired of being here, feel so much interest in the men under my charge. The friends of men who have died seem so grateful to me for the little that it was in my power to do for them. I saw a man die in half a minute from the effects of chloroform; there is nothing that has affected me so much since I have been here; it seems almost like deliberate murder. His friends arrived today but he had to be buried before they came. Every kind of distress comes upon the friends of soldiers.

We have a nice table, meals regularly, and the nicest roast beef every day, cornbread too.

To think there is not one of the men under my care that can get up yet! How patient they are though, never complain and lay still from day to day—how different from sick men at home. I am published on the walls of the tent as the "Lady-nurse." All kinds of conversation go on here every day, a great deal of it is just like Bill

19

Buchalew used to talk. Tell father that I have my shoes greased and do everything in army style.

From thy daughter,

C. HANCOCK

[From her Cousin Isabel]

Salem, N. J., Aug. 10, 1863.

MY DEAR CORNELIA

YOUR letter reached me in Bridgeton, where I was spending a few days with my friend. I was glad to find that you were still doing so well. I imagine you must be nearly out of calico gowns, so Sarah sent you one in the box we fixed before I got off. I could not have the satisfaction of seeing it closed for some of the aid work was not finished, but I did my part and I trust before this you have received it. William was in on Saturday and told me Ellen had been on to clothe you or I should have gone today about the strong calico. I would have got it directly but knowing the other had gone I thought you would not need it immediately, so finished my visit. You need not have mentioned the money. Albeit I'm generally pretty close to the wind these days I could give a *calico* to my suffering sister and consider it done for the soldiers if you choose. If I do not go myself I feel it my duty to *do* at home. We sent some delightful boxes from here. I trust they reached their destination. Did you get the stamps I sent? Morris is getting on quite well with his recruiting. Henry is home ill, but intends going to Bridgeton again soon for the double purpose of overseeing the church he is building there and assisting in the recruiting. What have you done with Mrs. Farnum? You never mention her. Are you sleeping in an open tent with no women near you? I cannot tell from your letter, but I trust not. I am glad your health keeps so good. Good-bye. Write soon and if you want anything let me know and I will try to send it.

Your affectionate cousin,

ISABEL

20

Camp Letterman, Aug. 23rd, 1863.

MY DEAR MOTHER

THE first best thing to say is that I received the barrel of things, all safe and all of them, even the dishcloths. I have seen those barrels and taken a reasonable amount of interest in them but this one coming from home seemed to me the nicest one I ever saw. Things in Government care carry very slowly, but, in my case, sure. The sheets were most valuable and came in time for Sunday inspection, I expect I took the prize again. I did last week. I always take my full share from the hospital store and then have my own to fill up the deficiency. Besides your barrel I received a large box from cousin Eleanor —it was splendid, fine shirts, drawers, cologne, rags and new sheets. They came Saturday, in time for Sunday inspection too. In it was a small box filled with nice little things like needles, thread, tape, etc., which Belle and Sallie fixed up. Sara S—— sent me a dress too; that box would have been a great loss, but it carried perfectly safe. Remember me to Old Mary; if she were here she could earn a dollar per day washing for the ladies. Mrs. Holstein is matron-in-chief here. Mrs. Harris does not come around now. Miss Dix peeks in every week or two. There is one woman here who has the clothes department. They call her "General Duncan"; she is the terror of the whole camp. She came and blew me up sky high for having my ward so clean, said I must get more than my share of clothes. I answered her very politely and held my tongue. I can get along with her if any one can.

If Charleston falls will we not begin to see our way through this war? I do not read the papers very often now, think I am doing all I can and leave the issue to God. I think war is a hellish way of settling a dispute. Oh, mercy, the suffering! All the worst are dying rapidly. I saw one of my best men die yesterday. He wore away to skin and bone, was anxious to recover but prayed he might find it for the best for him to be taken from his suffering. He was the one who said if there was a heaven I would go to it. I hope he will get there before I do. He was not in my ward now, but I just went over in time to be with him when he died. I hope to keep well enough to

21

stay with the men I am now with until they are all started on their way to heaven or *home*.

It is very interesting getting them started on crutches. They are so patient, they never bother for anything; they are jolly even, for the most part.

It is great fun to prop yourself up with pillows on a nice little iron bedstead and write letters home. Sergeant Hart has given me one of the best gold pens and it writes so nicely.

From thy daughter,

CORNELIA HANCOCK

[From Jeff Davis, an Ambulance Driver]

Morris Ville, Va.
August 23rd, 1863.

TO MISS HANCOCK

IT is Sunday Evening and so I think that I would write a few lines to you about the Army—they was a man shot here today. He was in the 71st Pennsylvania—he was an awful brave man—he walked from the General's headquarters to where his grave was and then the officer in charge of the men who was to shoot him told the men to stand back then he put a bandage around his eyes then told him to get down on his coffin—he did so then the officer read the orders and asked the man if he was ready—the man said that he was, the officer told the men to fire. I fore wone do not want to see another man shot but I did not want to see him shot but I had to. Dr. Dwinell have got back to the corps—we have got a pleasant place to encamp the third division is not with the corps—it is at some station doing guard duty I believe. Dr. Jones have got back and some of the boyes that was with you—we will lay hear fore some time if the Rebels do not disturb us—did Miss Lee stay with you. I seen Miss Jane Moore the other day at the depot she was in wone of the 12th army corps ambulance—how meny wounded is they there now out of the 2nd corps—we had a brush with the Rebels but they didn't wound meny of their

22

boyes so I heard. I can't think of any more at present. If there is anything that I can do for you please let me no and I will do it—tell Bracket that I will write to him soon—did Miss Lee get her mettle how did it look? I must close good-night Miss H. write as soon as convenient and oblige

Your friend

JEFF DAVIS

Ambulance train 2nd division 2nd corps

Camp Letterman, Gen. Hospital
near Gettysburg, Pa. Aug. 31st, 1863.

MY DEAR SISTER

THOSE who write to me will get written to. I received thy letter. To-day is Sunday. It seems more like one than any that has ever passed since I came here. It is a perfect day. All the men in my ward are doing well but two. Rufus M. is in process of dying. He belongs to the 111th, New York, had keen black eyes and laid in the upper tent where thee saw him. I have taken every care of him that is possible; was determined to save him, his leg has commenced bleeding and he cannot last long. Weatherlow was amused at thy sending him the handkerchief. He is doing middling well. He is one who is very anxious to see Doctor. Mary S. spent the day out here and I tried in every way to make her visit interesting. I have written a long letter for the Penn Relief, but descriptions on paper seem so tame to me. It seems hardly worth sending. Thee can judge of that and send it or not. I want John to copy it. I like Mrs. Holstein real well. I am most too smart for her. I *will* get the things for the men without orders and she is a great respector of order. I am considered the shiftiest woman on the ground. I like it real well here. I am all dressed up nice and clean, feel pretty well and sitting on a nice iron bedstead and we live in good style now—thus far I had written when dinner came; thought what a nice day we were going to have, went into the ward

23

and found two men deathly sick. Have been running faithfully ever since and it is now nine at night. We had the medical director around yesterday, had a big inspection; he was a real alive man, went with the surgeon in charge of this hospital, went into every tent, pointed to every man, asked him the point blank question "Do you get enough to eat?" The men, of course, answered in the negative. Then in the presence of Chamberlain said: "The first thing to set your self about is feeding these men; there is nothing better, *feed them*, I say, feed them. Feed them till they can't complain." Said he had been in the service twenty-five years. Said *he* could feed men till they would not complain. Said clean avenues and clean tents would not cure a man. Things were better today and they will be, I know. The old gentleman stuck his head in every oven, in the barrels, into everything and is still on hand. The boys gave three cheers for Cuyler after dinner today. I have a great curiosity to see my Sesesh watch, wanted that sent in place of the gold one but was thankful for any, they are invaluable in camp. I think thee would enjoy visiting the hospital. Thee could stay all night here, eat at a nice table and see a splendid camp hospital.

from thy sister,

C. HANCOCK

Send me stamps. Collect money if you can. I could buy butter.

Philadelphia, Sunday, Sept., 1863.

MY DEAR MOTHER

I SUPPOSE thee has heard through Mary Shourds that Doctor was going to Gettysburg and that I was coming home with him. The hospital got so full of women that one had to sit down while the others turned round, so I thought the most patriotic one was she who took her board off of Uncle Sam until there was greater need of services. It was very pleasant living in Camp Letterman and as soon as there is another battle, I shall go again. The boys say they will hollow "Miss Hancock" as soon as they fall. It will be awful to see the next

24

battle, for there are so many men that I know now, some of which will fall in the next fight.

The men are coming on to Philadelphia now, some every week, I cannot go into any hospital here without someone calls me by name. The Government paid me Nine dollars and sixty cents and passed me on the road free as a Government Nurse. So I am very little money out of pocket by this trip. We brought Col. Colville with us as far as Harrisburg. We strung his bed up by ropes, and let him swing like a rocking chair. I wish all the men could be carried with half the care, but the one great fact ever before ones eyes in the army—*he is an officer*. I carried his sword, one that he captured from a Rebel Major in the first Bull's Run fight, and which he has carried in every battle the Army of the Potomac has ever fought. He was one who went through Baltimore at the point of the Bayonet and has been on hand ever since; was slightly wounded at Antietam and laid very low at Gettysburg. All the family are well here except Doctor, he seems to have taken his Gettysburg experience very hard. The Second New Jersey Cavalry is to leave Trenton soon I believe. Morris was here to bid me good-bye yesterday. It does not seem to me anything to go to war now. I look upon it so differently, nothing seems to me like a hardship. A soldier's life is very hardening; you do not care where you are so you can eat and sleep. I had a tooth drawn the other day without flinching, said to myself, if I could not have a tooth drawn after all the suffering I had seen patiently borne, it was a poor story. My nerves are in a much more healthy state. If I was rich I should come down and see you, but I cannot afford to be running back and forth.

Philadelphia—October 3rd, 1863.
[After a visit home at Hancock's Bridge]

MY DEAR MOTHER

I LEFT rather unceremoniously, but I went to Salem and found five letters for me, one from Dr. Dwinelle, saying he had a hospital of

25

200 sick at Culpeper, and I thought I would write to him and ask him if he needed help there. I am now awaiting his answer. I send a letter enclosing one he sent first. I expect I shall get another soon. There must be terrible suffering at Chatanooga, but I think the Western ladies ought to help them. I get very nice letters from the men who are still in Gettysburg; they got the box all safe that I sent them.

C. HANCOCK

[From a Soldier at Gettysburg]

Camp Letterman, Sept. 28th, 1863.

DEAR MISS HANCOCK

I RECEIVED your very affectionate letter addressed to the Boys generally, and if you could have been here and seen the attention they paid while reading your letter to them you would be ever proud of them for they will never forget their ministering angel. The weather was fine for the Picknic, the viands were good and the boys laid hold as if the food was exactly to their taste. They appeared to enjoy themselves; as for me I relished everything, not a word of complaint could I utter, the soup was good, likewise the butter; we are pleased to learn that you were surrounded by christians in your Travels and that you had the attention paid as a "distinguished Traveller"—it is an unison of feeling that we call you such. We are all getting along finely. Quiggin is much better. Haynes seems the very impersonation of Physical ease and good nature; the sergeant gets his leg lanced. You would hardly know the camp the tents are ornamented and decorated, so suffice that I will not know myself if I do not quit writing very soon. The men speak volumes of the nobleness of your generous Heart in sending them such excellent butter and cake and other things too numerous to mention; some of us expect to go to Philadelphia this week, they are breaking up camp very fast. I have to look twice to see Gid Durfey he gets in such a small Heap, he keeps that good natured grin on his face. Since I have nothing more

26

of importance to write I will quit. I am a very poor communicant at best, so adieu God Bless you, you generous soul—is the prayers of us all.

Very respectfully, your obedient Servant

W. H. H.

III

CONTRABAND: WASHINGTON

✿

Philadelphia—October 13th, 1863.

MY DEAR MOTHER

I REPORT myself again though I did not expect so to do until I was safe down in Dixie. I did expect to start tonight for Washington, but this morning Dr. Burmeister called to see me to say all the hospitals had been brought in from the front to Washington. When he left Dr. Dwinelle, his orders were to bring me back with him, but the aspect of things has changed somewhat so that his advice was to hold on until they could write to me. Things are gloriously uncertain in the military world. James Gasgill advised me to apply to some of the Bankers of this city to aid me in an outfit for my present employment. I did so, and the result was I got fifty dollars without any trouble. Jay Cooke gave me Twenty Dollars—he is the 5–20 loan man. Clark & Drexel gave me ten dollars each and two others gave me five dollars each—it seems a very easy way to get money. I have bought and made myself two suits of strong clothing—shoes, leggings and everything complete, and am ready in body and mind to start any time. Things are almost a fabulous price. I do not think I could possibly have bought things enough to have made myself comfortable if I had not got in with the Brokers. I do not think I would mention it *out* that I got that money—rightly represented it is a perfectly legitimate matter, but things get so grossly misrepresented by repetition. The war news is not very cheering at present. The news looks more like a general battle, but I hope it will not be one for I know our forces are not capable of a general rout of the Rebels and drawn battles. . . . I received a very nice letter from R. D. Owen, Ambassador to Italy,

28

recommending me to favor any where in Washington. He is coming here this week. I am going to ask him if he cannot give me something in Washington to do for the contrabands until Dr. Dwinelle sends for me again. All are well here. From thy daughter,

CORNELIA HANCOCK

Philadelphia—October 25th, 1863.
I HAD expected to receive a letter from some of you this week but have not. As I am going away tomorrow, I will write you. I expect to go to Washington tomorrow night, start at twelve, will get into Washington about eight on the third day morning. I am going to see Janet Jackson, who is on Georgetown Heights with a home for Colored orphans; she is on one of the confiscated country seats, George Cox's. I do not know her very well, but I am tired of staying in Philadelphia doing nothing, when I know there is much to be done for both contrabands and soldiers. Just as soon as the army is settled, I shall go to the Second Corps Hospital and before then I shall support myself in Washington in some way, either working for contrabands or soldiers, I do not care which. Mr. Owen is visiting here now; he read to us a speech that he read to the President one Sunday. It was as clear a piece of composition as I ever listened to. The subject was the Pardoning Power Vested in the President. He said that Abraham listened with all his attention, then asked if he would give it to him, and also had him promise he would not have it published for the present; said he would read and consider it well. Complimented Mr. Owen, told him he had been of much service to him in many ways. Mr. Owen says he is sorry to find that Sec. Chase has the Presidential fever. He really is the most interesting homely man I ever saw. . . .

Washington, D. C.—October 29th, 1863.
MY DEAR SISTER
I SENT you one letter yesterday, perhaps it fell into that place from whence letters are never issued, so I write you this to tell my where-

29

abouts. I stayed the first night with Miss Mann, the next day Janet and I went into town. We went to see Mrs. Swisshelm who is in government employ in the Quartermaster Department, and has nothing whatever to do with hospitals. The first thing she said to me, after I told her I had been on duty in the hospital, was she was glad to see I was *not* seventy years of age. She is truly an old woman. . . . We went to Dr. Breed's—there I was met with a very cordial welcome. Mrs. Breed is a woman of very fine character indeed and wonderfully interested in the contrabands. She asked me to stay at her house. She keeps two horses and a carriage and took me out to the camp. She is very anxious I should get into business there and until I do, I can stay with her. She does everything right and properly. But party feeling runs very high here among different people who are engaged in contraband service. Dr. Breed's people belong to the Owen faction. . . . They want me to take charge of the hospital,—(for contraband). It is old hospital strife right over again only intensified on account of the women being smarter. Little Menah Breed and I went to the White House this morning, and I told you I would encounter the President—sure enough, there he stood talking to some poor woman. I did not stop him because he was in a hurry, but I know him now and I shall. It is a much easier matter to see *him* than Stanton. Stanton lives right opposite Mrs. Breed's. They are to give me an answer whether they will receive my services tomorrow morning. Mrs. Breed is so kind to me. I shall work while I am in Washington for her contrabands even if I could get a situation among the soldiers. But I do not think I can leave the Third Division boys when they have a hospital established—even for the contrabands. Dr. Dwinelle's letter was awaiting me—I will enclose it. He will be likely to send for me if he establishes a hospital anywhere. I would like you to send this letter to mother as it will save me writing to her for the present. I consider myself very lucky in getting in with Mrs. Breed, and Mr. Owen's letter helped me to that very much. I am glad I came even if I do not get a situation, for it is "Another phase of Life," as

30

Mrs. Farnham says. No tidings from the Second New Jersey, and it does seem to me as if I had seen a few of every regiment there is around, too. I hope to get a letter from some of you this day.

C. HANCOCK

Contraband Hospital, Washington.
Nov. 15th, 1863.

I SHALL depict our wants in true but ardent words, hoping to affect you to some action. Here are gathered the sick from the contraband camps in the northern part of Washington. If I were to describe this hospital it would not be believed. North of Washington, in an open, muddy mire, are gathered all the colored people who have been made free by the progress of our Army. Sickness is inevitable, and to meet it these rude hospitals, only rough wooden barracks, are in use—a place where there is so much to be done you need not remain idle. We average here one birth per day, and have no baby clothes except as we wrap them up in an old piece of muslin, *that* even being scarce. Now the Army is advancing it is not uncommon to see from 40 to 50 arrivals[1] in one day. They go at first to the Camp but many of them being *sick* from exhaustion soon come to us. They have nothing that any one in the North would call clothing. I always see them as soon as they arrive, as they come here to be vaccinated; about 25 a day are vaccinated. This hospital is the reservoir for all cripples, diseased, aged, wounded, infirm, from whatsoever cause; all accidents happening to colored people in all employs around Washington are brought here. It is not uncommon for a colored driver to be pounded nearly to death by some of the white soldiers. We had a dreadful case of Hernia brought in today. A woman was brought here with three children by her side; said she had been on the road for some time; a more forlorn, wornout looking creature I never beheld. Her four

---

[1] Released slaves.

31

eldest children are still in Slavery, her husband is dead. When I first saw her she laid on the floor, leaning against a bed, her children crying around her. One child died almost immediately, the other two are still sick. She seemed to need most, food and rest, and those two comforts we gave her, but clothes she still wants. I think the women are more trouble than the men. One of the white guards called to me today and asked me if I got any pay. I told him no. He said he was going to be paid soon and he would give me 5 dollars. I do not know what was running through his mind as he made no other remark. I ask for clothing for women and children, both boys and girls. Two little boys, one 3 years old, had his leg amputated above the knee the cause being his mother not being allowed to ride inside, became dizzy and dropped him. The other had his leg broken from the same cause. This hospital consists of all the lame, halt, and blind escaped from slavery. We have a man & woman here without any feet theirs being frozen so they had to be amputated. Almost all have scars of some description and many have very weak eyes. There were two very fine looking slaves arrived here from Louisiana, one of them had his master's name branded on his forehead, and with him he brought all the instruments of torture that he wore at different times during 39 years of very hard slavery. I will try to send you a Photograph of him he wore an iron collar with 3 prongs standing up so he could not lay down his head; then a contrivance to render one leg entirely stiff and a chain clanking behind him with a bar weighing 50 lbs. This he wore and worked all the time hard. At night they hung a little bell upon the prongs above his head so that if he hid in any bushes it would tinkle and tell his whereabouts. The baton that was used to whip them he also had. It is so constructed that a little child could whip them till the blood streamed down their backs. This system of proceeding has been stopped in New Orleans and may God grant that it may cease all over this boasted free land, but you may readily imagine what development such a system of treatment would bring them to. With *this* class of beings, those who wish to do good to the contrabands must labor. Their standard of morality is very low.

Contraband Hospital—Washington
November 17th, 1863.

MY DEAR SISTER

. . . It certainly seems strange to speak of a party in these times, but I am very glad every one does not feel called upon to act as I do, nor to know of the manifold suffering I have beheld. Do not let it excuse you from sending children's and babies' clothing, that you have it not on hand. Call an especial meeting and send some. If you could see the hordes of people in need, I do not think you would delay: while the weather is moderate, they do not suffer, but the first cold day, woe betide them! I almost hate to wear my good warm clothing; they look at my warm sack and say they wish they had one like it. If thee had seen R. Moore, thee would have met with a very loquacious lady. I do not know whether she knows where I am or not; it was talked of while she was here, but the Surgeon here then did not need help. But as he told me by word of mouth that he had no objection to my coming, I went and had a conversation with the Surgeon-General Barnes. He said appointments were made altogether on the Surgeon-in-charge. So I told Dr. Powell if he did not personally forbid my coming, I should come, for I had made it all right with the Surgeon-General. He said, very well, so here I am. I get on very well with Dr. Powell, he is part Indian—a good doctor, not extra for planning. But I tell you I have put this hospital right through. He lets me do pretty much as I please. The only thorn in my flesh is the colored matron, who was here before me. She is acting up some but I am in hopes of getting things straightened out with her, for she is a smart woman for some things. There is no use informing me anything in regard to hospital matters, for I am posted. The Surgeon-General told me of that order before it was published, particularly called my attention to the marked phrase—said that he both could and would appoint ladies at the request of a surgeon *irrespective* of *age, size* or *looks*, merely at the *request* of a Surgeon-in-Charge. He said that was particularly inserted to allow surgeons to choose their *own* nurses, as many objected to Miss Dix's.

33

Contraband Hospital
Washington, Dec. 19th, 1863.

MY DEAR WILLIE [1]

THY letter was received. It gave a very good description of the occupations of the other children. I find thee has commenced to go up in thy school which is good.

Have you had your charades yet?

I hope you will fix it so as to *make some money* at it, to buy some warm clothing for the shivering contrabands. Thee need to feel very glad thee was not born a contraband for lots of them have nothing to wear but a little thin frock and not a very warm house to sleep in. Henry Smith I guess has got so far away thee hardly knows Geography enough to find it on the map, Eastport, Mississippi. He is at least warm there, which is more than he would be in the Army of the Potomac. Thy playthings were very satisfactory. Menah Breed is busy making paper horns to hold candy and I guess she will make some for me. She is a very nice little girl that knows the way about Washington as well as thee does in Philadelphia. I carried 7 little contrabands to the orphans' Asylum today. I found them in the old hall, all cold and hungry with bare feet and no clothes on them scarcely. They had had nothing to eat for some time except their suppers last night which I gave them in the hospital. I put them into an ambulance and carried them down to Dr. Breed's and they will take them to the Home tonight, and I feel very sure they are much better off than they were last night.

AUNT CORNELIA

Contraband Hospital—
Washington, Dec. 23rd, 1863.

MY DEAR MOTHER

I RECEIVED a letter from thee dated 13th of 12th month, thought most thee had forgotten me. That Phil[a] Freedman Relief does not send

[1] Her nephew.

34

much to Washington for contrabands. They ought to buy yarn and knit some large stockings. The government stockings are not large enough for the contrabands; their feet are just exactly like hoofs and cut right through their stockings. It is almost impossible to keep them supplied—I have no doubt the Decade Meeting was very interesting but when you see the men who have charge here you could not help thinking where are all those good abolitionists north that do so much *talking* and so little *acting* . . . I think in a short time I shall go down to the Army. The camp here was torn down this week and the people were ordered to Arlington but out of 700 not more than 100 went over the river, the rest are packed in with their friends in the little huts around—just as thick as bees. They can not so maintain themselves and will have to go to Arlington before long. Meanwhile they bother me to know what the "govrnor" (government) is going to do with them. Such ignorance no where reigns as among contrabands. They will hang on to a white person as their only hope.

I went out last night and fed one dozen that I found that had nothing to eat all day. One woman brought her children to me and told me to take them as she could not keep them alive any longer. So I got an ambulance and hunted up seven and took them to the orphans' asylum. Emily Howland is here now. I like her very much. I want to attend Congress when Ellen comes down. The Sanitary Commission is worth its weight in gold. They certainly have got together a humane and noble set of men to execute its business—and that class of men in Washington is so scarce.

Willie's playthings have come for the children and some candy so I hope to make them feel Christmas—some. . . . Christmas day has passed. We had a Christmas tree for the children and gave every one in the hospital plum pudding for dinner. It was beautiful weather. Some of the contrabands entertained themselves fighting and generally seemed to have a good time.

I received a letter dated 19th of 12th Mo. today—it was long and interesting. I think the letters carry very well considering the num-

35

bers mailed from this city. I cannot find out whether William is enlisting white soldiers or black?

Our hospital accommodates 150 patients, consists of two buildings, a female and a male ward, and the officers quarters, the mess house and kitchen run along at the head (at right angles). It is good new barracks. All the money you would be likely to collect make into yarn stockings, large size for men, in fact any kind of stockings, but if men's very large—their feet are so much larger than common people's. You could not do better than send your box to the Sanitary Commission people for they do business just right. And it would amount to just the same thing as sending it to me for they give me anything I want even for the contrabands and of course they would for the soldiers. They always treat me well; so do the Christian Commission though too. I have no trouble getting anything I want. But the trouble with the contrabands is keeping things after you get them. To give out clothing is like pouring water through a sieve—you never see it again.

What has become of my secesh watch? I always see the Anti-Slavery Standard but the Salem Standard does not appear yet. This sending delegates to *visit* a few days in a vicinity is not what I consider the best plan to find out facts. I know if I had come to Washington and looked around a few days I should not have been competent to have rendered any kind of an account of them. The best way for a society is to send a delegate who is active and persevering right to the *spot* to labor, and let them communicate by letter, then the truth will be gained—not unless.

I can now appreciate why the Stewarts do not make any account of death—simply because they are used to it. I am perfectly convinced I do my duty in regard to writing whatever may be said to the contrary. I *do not* wish a comfortable sent to me, only my leggins—give my love to all the friends,

From thy daughter,

CORNELIA HANCOCK

36

Contraband Hospital, January 4th, 1864.

MY DEAR SARAH [1]

. . . IT seems from your own description that your part of the country [New Jersey] is one vast hospital. Things in general seem to move in your quarter just as usual—the Methodists celebrate struggling to escape the draft, etc.—They have issued an order here preventing any black man going north but the large bounties offered in Massachusetts, $325. induces them to go north on the underground R.R. and get the bounty. They offer me $5 for every volunteer I can secretly obtain. I expect William would enter into it with zest if he were here. I shall get them if I can with what time I have for they draft them here and compel them to go for nothing, and I am interested for them that they should enlist from Massachusetts. I think black regiments from that state are better treated than District soldiers.

I should very little fear all the small pox you may be likely to have in Salem after standing over it so long here. Last Sunday an ambulance drove up to the guard and dumped down some five children right upon the ground. They had been discharged from Kalorama [smallpox] hospital, all of them sick and sore. The poor little things did not know what to do and at first I did not know either, but I took them to a shanty near by and got some beds from the small pox tents and put them to bed. Dr. Powell visits them and they are doing very well. The poor little things would have surely died if they had not met with me, or some kind friend. When they get well I shall send them to the Orphans' Asylum. I could make much use of thee if I had thee here. I should be sorry to have thee exposed to the diseases I am, otherwise it would be good discipline in patience and perseverance. . . . I hope Salem Co. will send one box to the Contrabands and I would be very glad that mother and Ann be the instigators of the gift. I shall stay here all winter if no suitable opportunity offers to do good among our soldiers or something unforeseen occurs here.

[1] Her niece.

37

. . . I live in a building just like our barn, with lath nailed over the cracks. Would you not think it hard to be put out there to sleep? All in use. A barn like ours in Washington, would be rented to Contrabands for $100 a year. For a room as large as our kitchen they have to pay $6 per month, yet when you tell them of the difference in the prices nothing would induce them to go North. I never could have known that people could keep body and soul together and be so ignorant as these people if I had not been an eye witness to it so long. I am so sleepy I can hardly see so must close, with love to all the family, I remain thy affectionate

Aunt

CORNELIA HANCOCK

Contraband Hospital, Jan. 20th, 1864.

MY DEAR MOTHER

I RECEIVED a letter from thee dated the 9th. Ellen has been and gone, had a very good visit except that she caught cold and her face swelled very much. It could hardly be expected that she could make such a journey in the depths of winter, live as I do for a week and not catch cold. I went everywhere with her—President's levee, Congress, Alexandria, Arlington, etc. Saulsbury has a very poor time this winter, when they get Gurit Davis expelled he will have very little company. His principal end in Congress appears to be to catch some of the Republican Senators in saying this war is being waged for the abolition of slavery. One of the senators jumped up and told him he had no hesitation in saying he (Saulsbury) was a *pro slavery* man. Sherman of Ohio is a very fine looking man. It is much more satisfactory to read the proceedings of the House than to be listening. It is the most disorderly place imaginable. The Senate is much better. Sumner is the handsomest man in the Senate. I had a conversation with him; he says the freedman's bureau will be established; says I must not be in a hurry, all things are coming round right. Ashley, M. C., from Ohio is my pattern man. He says he will swear, or affirm, that I am loyal, or do anything I want. I have been offered the situation of

38

matron in the hospital at Arlington with a salary of $20 per month. But they are just now investigating the rascality of a man by the name of Nichols who is superintendent in chief at Arlington. I want they shall get all the vultures out and start fresh before my name is connected with the establishment. I have no fear if I want to stay but that I can find places enough where they will be glad to have me. I shall stay just where I am unless Mrs. Lee comes to Washington to go to the army, then I will go with her. I went to hear Anna Dickeson lecture in the House of Representatives. She did what not one half the Congressmen do, made every one hear every word distinctly. She was dressed quite plainly and spoke very well, but her talents certainly lie in the pathetic and dramatic direction.

I was sick yesterday for the first time since I have been in Washington—had fever and a chill, but am up today and feel much better. It is a miracle how any one can have prolonged good health in such a neighborhood. I suppose 10,000 rats would hardly cover the number that have lain unburied in our immediate vicinity for nearly one month when at the same time we have had a guard of 40 white soldiers and more contrabands than you can count. But both classes of people are untoward lazy. The consequences are that we live in a state of filth that to mention in civilized society would be disbelieved utterly.

January 22nd

. . . What would you think of my going to Benedict, Maryland to General Birnly's division to be in a hospital there? They have a very large hospital; the surgeons are the only ones around who can read well enough to administer medicine. . . . The lives of black *soldiers* are more account to the U. S. than these contrabands around Washington. The more of them the Lord gathers to himself the better I feel, provided they do not suffer too much in the process of moving. I know there is a great need for me to stay where I am while the surgeon is as neglectful as now, but could he be removed and a good one in his place the need for me would subside; and I do not think I can put up with his conduct much longer. If I go to the

39

Medical Director of this post and tell him what I know of Powell he certainly would have to leave his post. I take everything easy, expect what is right will take place and do as much as I can each day, and when the great day of reckoning comes when the herds of people have to answer for their sins committed upon soldiers and contrabands, I hope I shall be one who will not meet condemnation. I do know some that must meet a just reward sometime or else there is no justice in heaven nor earth. I speak strongly; but it is true it takes two good persons to watch one knave and then he can accomplish more evil than the two can overthrow in a long time. New York Friends are here investigating the conduct of men who have had charge of contrabands here. They find a sort of second hand slavery has been going on some time.

Emily Howland is all about. I have not made up my mind in regard to her yet. Her field of operation is some distance and I have not had a good opportunity to see her performances. . . .

If I did not dislike to travel so much I could come home any time to stay a short time but I do not suppose I shall come very soon. From thy daughter

CORNELIA HANCOCK

Jan. 1864.

DEAR WILLIAM [1]

WHERE are the people who have been professing such strong abolition proclivity for the last thirty years?—certainly not in Washington laboring with these people whom they have been clamoring to have freed. They are freed now or at least many of them, and herded together in filthy huts, half clothed. And, what is worse than all, guarded over by persons who have not a proper sympathy for them.

I have been in the Washington Contraband Hospital for the past two months—it is in close proximity to the Camp of Reception—and I have had ample opportunity to see these people, the persons in charge of them, and the whole mode of proceeding with them. Their

[1] Her brother.

40

wants are great and appeal in every way for aid from the North. Their idea of freedom is exemption from labor. And those who are industrious and do labor we find much neglected on the part of employers in paying. Consequently there is much less inducement for them to labor than there otherwise would be. To get them to labor is the earnest desire of everyone working for the interest of these people—for they *must* be self-supporting—they should not remain paupers upon the government as they now are. They are totally ignorant of the mere rudiments of learning, not one in one hundred can read so as to be understood. The laws were very stringent in the slave states on that subject. A night patrol visited every cabin to see if they were using any books. Many of them kept their books in leather bags between the logs of their houses so as to escape detection, and after the patrol had been around took them down and endeavored through fear and trembling to learn something. . . .

The situation of the Camp is revolting to a degree, 12 or 14 persons occupy a room not 15 ft. square, do all their cooking, eating, etc. therein. The Camp has but one well of water and that out of order most of the time. All the water used by nearly 1,000 persons is carted from Washington so one can judge of the cleanliness of the Camp.

In "the hall," consisting of nothing conducive to comfort, neither light nor beds, probably some fifty sleep and the consequence is in a few days several of these people are seized with some aggravated disease and have to be carried to the hospital on stretchers and lay there to be supported by this same government that the authorities here say refuses to give them better accomodations when they first arrive. Now, I maintain an ounce of preventative would be worth a pound of cure, if the object is to save the government expense.

The Hospital here is under the care of colored surgeons. It was built under the supervision of Dr. Breed of Washington, and is supplied just as other hospitals are. It is the most humane establishment for the accomodation of contrabands that there is in Washington. We have here all sick and wounded black soldiers, all sick servants serving officers in the army, and the sick in general around Wash-

41

ington. Smallpox has raged here to a great extent but a separate hospital has been established for that now. The order now is to remove all contrabands south of the Potomac. It may be better there than here, but we remain under the same authority and let me state emphatically that nothing for the permanent advancement of these people can be effected until the whole matter is removed from the military authority and vested in a separate bureau whose *sole object* is the protection and elevation of these people.

Now this whole contraband business is under military regulation and under officers that think to spend government money for *contrabands* all waste. Now I can *see* the abuses here plainly but to *remedy* them is the trouble. Many wise and good people visit here and exclaim "*this must not be*," go away fully convinced they will do all in their power to rectify matters; go to some *military* functionary, who probably cares as little and less for a contraband than his riding horse. *He* informs them all is done for contrabands that the government allows; *so* you might go to numerous military men and receive the same answer. I say all is *not* done for contrabands that government allows. The designs of the government are not carried out by subordinate authorities. And the only way to ever get justice done to these people is to separate the whole matter from the military authority, make a separate bureau, have men at the head of this bureau with living souls in them large enough to realize that a contraband is a breathing *human being* capable of being *developed*, if not so now. Let them have the power to appoint officers to have charge of these camps, good energetic, anti-slavery persons who will take an interest in the improvement of those under their charge. I feel this to be the duty of every individual to urge upon every senator and congressman that this step be taken, but meanwhile as we stand at present, our needs are very pressing and any contributions of any kind of clothing, old or new, shoes and stockings especially, both men's and women's, will prevent much immediate suffering. There is much charity being extended to our poor soldiers and I would not that any one should withhold one mite from them, but I maintain that persons living in their comfortable homes in the North should give liberally to those so sadly situated as these forlorn contrabands, as well as to the soldiers. A national Sanitary Commission for the Relief of Colored Persons of this class would save lives and a great deal of suffering. The slaves generally get free when our army advances; they come into our lines several hundred at a time, follow the army for a while, then come into Washington, some probably having walked 50 miles. One woman carried one child in her arms and dragged two by her side. Judge of the condition of that woman when she arrives. Should not some comfortable quarters await her weary body?

Thy sister,
CORNELIA H.

Contraband Hospt.
Washington, Feb. 2

MY DEAR MOTHER

I RECEIVED a letter from thee dated January 21. Have just time to answer today. I am well and busy. I am teaching in the school here this week 2 hours in the day, and teach night school every other night, so you may readily see I am busy.

from thy daughter
CORNELIA HANCOCK

Washington, Feb. 2nd, 1864.

MY DEAR SARAH

I HEAR thee had the measles. I hope not badly. I wrote about one half dozen lines to Mother, but now that I have time I will write rather more explicitly. I wrote William a letter last week giving him a dissertation upon Contraband business in general. Aunt Beulah keeps me well posted in Beesly Neck news: she is capital upon letter writing. I ask no boot of anyone now I get the Salem paper and I know no great events will pass its eye unnoticed. What do you intend to buy at Grandmother's Vendue? Be careful about buying trumpery. I

43

would like to buy that little low chair that stood in the dining room. Do not buy that parlor carpet, it is so ugly; put our dining room carpet in the parlor and buy their dining room carpet.

I am going over to Arlington to see the hospital on Saturday next, maybe I will take up with the situation there of matron in the hospital; if so, I will get $20. per month and then I can send you money to buy some of Grandmother's things. Dr. Dwinelle wrote me a letter yesterday stating they had their Corps hospital established at last and no lady to take charge. I wrote if he would send a written request for my services I would try to secure a pass and go down. People say that it is very difficult for ladies to secure a pass to get to the Army, but my motto is "What is vigorously set about can generally be accomplished." Time will show, I do not live but from day to day. I never concern much about what will happen tomorrow. I have been teaching in school this week and you would be astonished at the little blacks. They know so much. They are very much smarter than the children of the people in our neighborhood who dislike them so much. I room in with a very nice young woman by the name of Miss Willetts, she comes from Jersey City. She is a teacher in school, used to be in the Camp next the hospital, but now that has been torn down we have a room together and she takes her meals at the hospital. If I do not go to the front and do go to Arlington hospital she is going there too to teach in the school and live in the hospital with me. She is one of the few that I have met with that suits my fancy.

Thy aunt CORNELIA

Washington, Feb. 5, 1864.

MY DEAR SISTER

I RECEIVED a letter from thee dated Jan. 31st. It was delayed in Mr. Holts hands, it and one from Col. Colville requesting me to come and see him at the National Hotel. I went, not expecting to find him, but did; he had had Reed out on the hunt for me but the contrabands that he met told him the hospital had been moved over the River—

44

true to their nature, stupid to the last. Col. said he had given out seeing me but seemed really delighted when he did. I always feel when in his presence, "here lies a brave man." He is confined to his bed, cannot put his foot to the ground yet. But his face looks as well as when first wounded. The way the senators and congressmen, judges and jury were paying honors to the colonel was gratifying in the extreme. His Regiment arrived in Washington from the front today and it is now the oldest Reg in the field. Tomorrow they are to have a dinner and Abe is to be out and a big time generally over them. They are going to Ft. Snelling, Minnesota to recruit and they are going to tote the Colonel along. He wishes to see Mrs. Lee and if she comes I will go again to see him. He wants I should come again but I shall not go unless she comes and wants to go. They leave here on Monday next. I was down to Dr. Breed's this evening to tea. Met with the "covenanters" who have come down with a mission among the contrabands. They seem like good men and I hope their first move will be to put up some buildings that can be rented in a *reasonable manner* since that is what they intend to try to do. I received a letter from Dr. Dwinelle a few days ago. He says they have a field hospital established at last which bids fair to be a first rate field hospital. They have three division surgeons in charge and Dr. Dwinelle has the supervision of the whole; says each division should have one female attendant—the cook's wife is in charge of 1st div. Dr. Aiken made a request for Mrs. Lee to come down and it met with approbation until it was taken to Gen. Warren; then he disapproved. Dr. Dwinelle said that would be the end of it but that Mrs. Lee would find it much more easy to get permission in Washington than down there. People say it is very difficult there but I do not know for I have not tried. I certainly shall go to the front if I can go with Mrs. Lee. Tonight is Saturday and no Mrs. Lee has appeared. I am going to write her another letter. Benjamin Latham, a Friend from New York city, has been here for some time investigating the character of Nichols' proceeding at Arlington, for the Secretary of War. Today he came up here in one of the stylish ambulances and invited me to go to Arlington with him. I accepted and Miss Willetts and I had a nice ride clear over to Camp Todd. The gentleman by the name of Janey, who was with Latham, was at Gettysburg and saw me there. That seems to have permanently established my reputation in this world. Benjamin Latham is a personal friend of Stanton's and Isaac Newton's, too. He told me if I wished to get a pass I might use his name to either of the gentlemen. I wish thee to know I have left the hospital. Miss Snowden hired two women and boarded one other to keep continually insulting me, and Dr. Powell had not energy enough to stop them. So I have left the whole party. I do not know what will become of the sick on their backs, but this thing I do know, that I stayed longer in that place than any other white person in the United States would have. I investigated into the Arlington hospital today but that looks so dreary no words can tell. But fortunately there were but 7 patients, so I did not bother my head about that. Now if Mrs. Lee appears I shall go with her; if not I shall stay exactly where I am and help the contrabands right in our neighborhood. Ever since the camp was broken up they know no place to go to get themselves coffins for their friends, or to get help, or a pass, and they wander to and fro in the most forlorn manner. They know me now and they want me to stay with them, so I shall. Sometimes they lay unburied for a week because there is no one to hunt up an order for them. The need of some one is acknowledged by all. I am here on the spot. They should not be the one to go into that business. All the trouble is we must have food. Miss Willetts boards at the hospital yet, but says she cannot stand it longer than this week. But she and I both feel very anxious to keep our room, we get along very nicely together and feel that this room is home to us. Now there is a talk that the Freedman's society in N. Y., Phila. and Washington are to join and make one National association; if so, they can be induced readily to pay me $25. a month to stay just as I am now. I am going to write to Margaret Griscom some time when I feel like it and explain matters to her. I do not want any money at present. Mr. Sperry pays me over a dollar a day for teaching in the school until they get a teacher

46

secured, so I am well off in the money line for the present. There is always a way provided for me to get along and I know for any one who tries to do his or her duty there always will be. I never look ahead one day for there is no certainty about anything in these diggings, so there is no use fretting. I am very well and contented. I hope you will not regret my leaving the hospital for I did stay just as long as I could.

from thy sister
CORNELIA HANCOCK

This is the 8th of February. I have lived in this world twenty-four years as thee probably knows. It is a most beautiful day here. I am going to teach school today. I went round to all the shanties yesterday—found many contrabands living (they say upon the Lord) without bread and almost naked. I do not go to the hospital now and have plenty of time to attend to their wants. Some one must do it. They must be sent to Arlington where the government can help them. The government does nothing for them on this side. Charity must attend to them or send them to Arlington.

If you send a colored person to an official in Washington, ten chances to one if they do not kick them out, and give them no satisfaction. So a white person has to go with them or write them an order.

47

IV

BRANDY STATION
VIRGINIA

✧

3rd Division, 2nd Corps Hospital
Washington
Feb. 10th, 1864.

DEAR MOTHER

I FEEL I must write thee a few lines to mail in Washington as I start for the Army of the Potomac tomorrow morning. Staunton has granted me a permanent pass to visit anywhere in the lines of the Union army, which I regard as a great favor. It will save me much vexation among his sub-officials. My medal secured it and it was presented to him by Senator Foster, a friend of mine introduced by Mrs. Peaco. Soon after I received my pass I received a request from a Surgeon, requesting me to come immediately as they had 150 wounded just brought in. I am tired tonight and shall close, hoping soon to write again and also to be preserved in good health, which I now enjoy. Direct letters in care of Dr. Dwinelle, Surgeon-in-Charge, 2nd Corps Hospital, near Brandy Station. Tell me what stores you have on hand for soldiers at present. Ann's and thy box were the most sensible things I have ever distributed to contrabands. I feel very much obliged to you for it. Give my love to Ann.

from thy daughter,

C. HANCOCK

48

Head Qtrs, 2nd Corps Hospt.
Brandy Station, Virginia
February 11th, 1864.

MY DEAR DOCTOR [1]

I WRITE to inform thee that I am once more in the presence of the wounded men of 3 Div. 2nd Corps hospital. Dr. Dwinelle looks very well, he has his wife here ensconced in a pleasant log house with a very cheerful fire blazing in the chimney corner. The hospital is beautifully laid out and far from forbidding in its aspect as it was at Gettysburg. The Head Qtrs. are tastefully adorned with evergreens and everything looks nice and clean. Dr. Dudley is in charge of Third Division, says he will have me a log house started tomorrow. The only thing now is for the Rebels to let us alone.

I had excellent success getting down here. The corduroy roads are awful in the extreme. We have no stove here is the only draw back I have seen yet. I have spent one day in the 3rd Div. If Dr. Dudley holds out as he has commenced he is first rate; he must be smart as he is a major Surg. and I should not think he was more than 23 years old. Dr. Dwinelle is going to have the corps hosp. photographed. Chard is about as numerous as ever, is hospital steward now. Today the men had for their breakfast oysters, meat and breads. For dinner, soup, Turkey broth, corn and lima beans. For supper oysters, farina, bread, and butter. So you see, although out of the world we are of the world. The men say they have not fared so sumptuously before and I guess that things have been suffered to collect and the stores may not hold out, but the ever present Sanitary and Christians are tented at Brandy Sta. so we shall be likely not to starve. The whole Potomac army stretches from Alexandria to Culpepper right on the line of the R. Road. I think there have been many over from the Regiments round; their sole purpose seeming to be to see a *lady*. After they take a good look they start back seemingly contented. I wish thee could see the hospital as it will be a week hence. It will be beautiful. Many of the men are badly wounded, principally of the

[1] Her brother-in-law, Dr. Child, with whom she went to Gettysburg.

49

Connecticut. Dr. Dudley is Surgeon of that Regiment. I feel as if I had got back home, it is as warm as spring here today and it has been a day of much satisfaction to me. Dr. Dudley says he will send to Washington and buy a stove for me. I never felt more relieved getting out of a place than Washington. How tired I got of it no words can express. Here I am sure I shall get fed free of expense and in Washington it cost, manage as you may, about $4. per week. Of course, there will be many disagreeable happenings but things look fair at present. Dr. Aiken is a nice man. I think Mrs. Lee is not flourishing yet until she gets a stove. I go down to the common cookhouse and cook on their stove. Mrs. Holstein would like to come down now. The cook's wife is the only lady except Dr. Potter's wife in 1st div. Dr. Dwinelle's wife is very much a lady. I feel so much better to think they sent me a positive request to come. Dr. Dudley did it upon a venture and, lo and behold! I had carried him grub on the Battlefield at Gettysburg, he was wounded in the shoulder there. I hope this will reach thee. I always answer letters sent to me and if you do not receive them it is not my fault. I send enclosed an old note I can do nothing with in Washington. It was sent to me from Dryden, Tompkins county, N. Y. to pay freight on a box for contrabands. Of course, I had to pay greenbacks to them and the note is useless to me. I am not out of money yet. I have to be very economical or I should be. I do not know more than this to write so with love to all the family I remain thy sister

CORNELIA HANCOCK

3rd Div. 2nd Corps Hospital
Feb. 13, 1864.

MY DEAR MOTHER

I TOLD you in Sallie's last letter you might hear from me almost any where and this is the place. I wrote thee a short letter saying I had received a permanent pass from the Sec. of War. I also received a letter from the Surg. in Charge of this hospital stating that he had

50

just received into this hospital one hundred and fifty wounded—to come on immediately if possible.

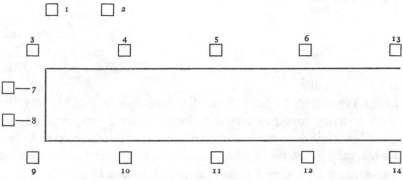

This is a rude plan of our hospital, 1 is dining room; 2 cook house; 3 hospital tent; 4 hospital tent; 5 hospital tent; 6 hospital tent; 7 wardmaster's tent; 8 steward's tent; 9, 10, 11, 12 hospital tent; 13 is where my log house is to be built; 14 Dr. Dudley's log house. The log houses are really complete. They build a nice chimney of clay, then two rooms of logs, one to sleep in and one for sitting in. Mrs. Lee is down here now. Dr. Dudley is very kind to me, says I can have anything on the ground, that all eatables are under my control. Every one must obey orders or punishment ensues very summarily indeed. The ink line in the diagram is a walk made of slabs split from logs and the sides bordered with cedar brush about half a yard high. I suppose I shall be home when the army moves this spring. We shall stay here and keep a hospital for the corps as long as the Rebs let us alone. This last skirmish killed and wounded about 250 of our men and did no good whatever. There are a great many ladies in the Army but they are mostly officers' wives. Dr. Dwinelle's wife is here, so is the Surg. in charge of the first Div. wife here, but it would be hard for Dr. Aiken of 2 division or Dudley of third to send for theirs, for they neither of them have any. Dr. Dudley is not a stranger to me. I carried him tobacco, he was wounded at Gettysburg. I did not know his name and supposed I would have to encounter a stranger but when

51

Dr. Dwinelle brought him in we both exclaimed Ah! we have met before! He wrote for me to come at Dwinelle's suggestion on a venture. I hope he will be satisfied.

thy daughter

C. HANCOCK

February 21st, 1864.

MY DEAR MOTHER

I HAVE not received a letter from thee for some time. There may be one wandering round somewhere though. They go to Brigade Head Qts. Gen. Hays knows me and marks them for the hospital and after a while they get to me. Today is the *21st* of February and I received a letter from thee. It was written evidently before I came down here or before thee knew it. I hope soon to hear from thee again. I believe I have written an account of my getting down here. Does thee remember how much Elizabeth wishes to live in a house of her own? I never realized how it was until now. I live in a house by myself and of *my own* emphatically. It was built especially for me and a very nice one it is. The first room is nearly as large as our dining room and the other room is large enough for a bed and a few chairs. I would like to entertain my family in it for a short time. I never felt the need of thee much in the Army until tonight. Dr. Dudley wanted some yeast made. He said he had hops. Is it possible to make yeast without any other yeast to raise it? I am experimenting tonight. I boiled the hops in water and scalded the flour and what it will be by morning I have no idea. We want it to make Indian meal poultice for erysipelas in wounded feet. One man is threatened with lockjaw tonight. I have just been talking with him. He seems cheerful. I do not think he is fully aware of his situation. I never was half as pleasantly situated in the army as now. The Surg. is a young man, very anxious to establish his reputation by curing bad cases; also he has some humanity, works just like William exactly. Works with his men just long enough to make him popular, then goes in and lies down on his bed and reads the paper. I think I am being paid now for my faithfulness among

52

THIRD DIVISION HOSPITAL

BRANDY STATION

(*Cornelia Hancock is the third figure on the extreme right*)

those contrabands. All I did there was nothing but one series of the most protracted self-denial. I was disliked by all the authorities, and the contrabands of course have always been used to see white people do for them and never expressed much enthusiasm. Here it is so different, everything I wish for, if wished aloud, is done instanter; any improvement I may suggest is listened to with attention. Dudley regards me as a help to him and the soldiers always feel relieved when there is one woman in a hospital, but not when there are *two*.

If you could only see my house; to think that the Rebs may occupy it sometime is all that troubles me. There is to be a ball given by the officers of the 2nd Corps tomorrow night. I have seven Washington ladies to entertain. I am glad it is warmer or I fear they would perish. I do not think any one here will attend it but we have such good quarters here, of course, we shall have to help entertain the ladies. Dr. Dudley says he will not go. I think though it will be hard for him to get out of it when it comes to the pinch. Dr. Dougherty, our corps inspector, wants to try to have Murdock, a celebrated reader, come down and use the room for him. If that is done I presume I shall be asked to go. You have no idea how many officers pass here in the course of a day. We are right in the woods and they ride in from every part. Gen. Webb was here today. There is only one official more who is needed here, that is someone to *escort visitors* around. Neither the Surg. or myself can bear the task and it is laughable what a skedaddling there is when visitors appear; but one of us has to take it. If it did not come so often it would not be so bad. Capt. Madison, 12th N. J. sent his compliments to me and said he would come over to see me. Gen. Hays who commands our division and who was so drunk in this last fight he could scarcely ride on his horse was here a few days ago. He is a very brave man, has a very nice wife indeed. Dr. Dwinelle has a very bad felon upon his hand. His wife is here. She is a *very nice* woman and if Dr. was not sick we should have such good times.

I had written thus far when I received thy other letter. I did receive the $5. what is it for? The contrabands, or is it my own?

53

Brandy Station is only about 40 miles from Washington. Thee need not be afraid while I keep within the *precincts* of the Army of Potomac that I will get *far* from that well guarded city. Thy mind can rest as easy as if I was in bed with thee. Mrs. Lee is about as far from me as over to Grandmother's. Dr. Potter's wife is here, so is Dr. Dwinelle's, all friendly, pleasant women. I would be extremely thankful to have the pads. I could distribute them here in about three days. They are sadly in need of them. The shirts I would not want. We have plenty and they are all woolen. If you would even send one dozen eggs and a pound of butter in with the pads I should be very glad. Those two articles are needed to a degree that is indescribable, also the plainest kind of cucumber pickles. I would give more for half barrel of cucumber pickles than almost anything you could send. Clothing is supplied so bountifully by the Sanitary Com that we scarcely know what want is in that particular. I want the *pads very badly*.

The Asst. Surg. in this hospital, is surg. of the 12 N. J. He is very much interested in the Salem paper, also all the 12 N. J. boys that are booming around the hospital. There is a man by the name of Gaskill around the hospital. I wonder if he is not one I have known. I will find out. He is a nice man.

I hope this letter will reach you. It has answered all thy questions and I hope will prove satisfactory.

from thy daughter
CORNELIA HANCOCK

It is now 20 minutes of 11 o'clock on the night of 21st of February, how old will father be tomorrow?

2nd Corps, 3rd Div. Hospital
Feb. 24th, 1864.

MY DEAR SISTER

I HAVE not received any letter from you very recently, but write tonight to inform you that my feet are nearly upon the ground and you will have to send me a pair of shoes pell mell or I shall have a cold. We do not have to go in the mud, however, as we have corduroy paths all the places to which I have to go. Dr. Dudley wants some silk handkerchiefs too and if he sends the money I suppose thee would get them. He has no family in the North to attend to him. His mother is in St. Augustine and sister at Port Royal. He is very kind to me. I am reaping my reward for my faithfulness in that contraband hospital. The 23rd was the Second Corps review. I would have liked to go to that, but all the ladies had to be got off and Dr. Dudley went too, so I stayed to keep the hosp. straight. If you could only see how we are fixed here, we are too inviting entirely; there is a perfect *lot* of ladies in the army and we have so much company. I would like the Sect. of war or any other secretary make laws strict enough to keep ladies out of any place. Mrs. Lee's daughter is here. I hope we shall be able to stay but such pleasant weather makes them look forward to a move. I hope the army will stand still forever myself. If it is not enough to sicken one to hear of the condition in which the officers lead our good men into these small fights. Gen. Warren's orderly is sick in hospital here, he says that he will not go on the field when he is drunk and the day of the last fight he could not get out of his Quarters until 4 o'clock. Gen. Hays meanwhile went splashing around on his own hook. I do not care what anyone says, war is humbug. It is just put out to see how much suffering the privates can bear I guess. Both doctors have gone over to the second div. to spend the evening. They wanted I should go but I had to write some letters and make beef tea so I did not go but am occupying their quarters because I can sit by the open fire. The 2nd Corps is undergoing a thorough inspection, all think here there is to be a move. Gen. Warren was here this morning.

Today is the 25th of the month. I have been troubled with the toothache. I am almost afraid I will have to go to Washington to have them filled. I hope not for that will cost awfully I expect. There is nothing of importance happening here: the drums beat, the bugle sounds, the winds blow, the men groan—that is all—

from thy sister, C. HANCOCK

55

You had better get some person to hem the handk as I do not want the bother and there is no one else to do it here.

3rd Div. 2nd Corps Hospt.
Near Brandy St., March 1st.

MY DEAR SISTER

I SENT a letter to thee requesting thee to send me a pair of shoes. For mercy sake do not delay my shoes. Miss W. gave away my morrocco shoes to contrabands in mistake. I am wretched when my feet are wet which they are now; this month it will rain all the time. I would give $10. instead of $5. if I had them now.

I am well, getting on first rate, peace and harmony dwell among us to a great extent so far; to get out of the strife of Washington is so refreshing to me.

from thy sister
CORNELIA HANCOCK

A colored man is now having both limbs amputated from the effects of small pox. Dr. Dudley says he will try my Abolitionism taking care of him. I think I will stand the test. He is down on the coloreds but always does his duty by his patients and will by him for the reason that he is a *patient.* He would not suit thee the way he talks, but he is young and may change before he dies.

3rd Div. 2nd Corps Near Brandy
March 2nd, 1864.

MY DEAR SARAH

I HAVE neglected writing to thee for sometime. I cannot write when I have received no letters and that I have not done for more than a week. I always feel lonesome as soon as I get no letters. You would wonder why anyone could feel lonesome here with so many around. They are very kind to me. My house is built and I live so comfortably comparatively speaking. I am now sitting in the Steward's tent up on two boxes with my feet on a pack of back logs, a bright log-fire burns in the fireplace right in front of me. A table filled with military

56

requisitions is beside me. The steward is a nice looking youth and is assisted by a man by the name of Toplis who is always making all kinds of odd speeches and under these circumstances I am endeavoring to write. Everybody swears here, if I do when I get home you need not be surprised. Scarce one exception, I do not think they attach any importance to it, just from habit. I wish you could see us here. It is quite an ordeal for any woman to come here and visit however; it would be if she *knew* all the remarks made about her as well as I hear them after they leave. I think I am particularly calculated for some reason or another to get on here. I do not feel as if I was half as useful as I did when at Gettysburg, but I like it much better; here there is order and not nearly the hard labor to perform. They are singing the most mournful tunes, some are beautiful singers here. Tonight must be the third of March. I think we have heard cannonading all day, but if it is in the distance we make no account of it whatever; just before night there was the report of something much nearer, but the unconcern with which the soldiers inquired about it! It did not alarm me. We know much less of the news here than if at home, for we only know what is *nearby* and do not get the paper until it is one day old. I have very easy times now, it would be an excellent time for me to take a furlough but I do not know how soon we shall be filled up here. Dr. said today he should send for the sick from the Regimental hospitals. I would like Joanna Dickeson to see how I am fixed here; if I had her opportunity I would see the Army of the Potomac, people North think it such a wonderful undertaking to visit the army. Why it is done by thousands of ladies, the army is filled with them! Sallie Ingham is going to send me $25. to purchase a stove that I can have with me in the army. She is a good girl and a true friend. My stove I have at present smokes; that is the most annoying thing I have to encounter. Dr. Dudley is far from being an Abolitionist, he has a little darkey who I think he treats very badly. I have frowned on his treatment so much that I think he has been doing better for the past few days, he is not cruel to him but makes him act the monkey and dance,

57

etc. which I do not like to see—just as Uncle Will does only on a larger scale. I am afraid I shall call Dr. Dudley "William" sometime for he certainly is like him—

From thy AUNT CORNELIA

3rd Div. 2nd Corps Hospital, Brandy, Va.
March 2, 1864.

MY DEAR MOTHER

I HAVE had a dinner company at which Dr. Dwinelle and his wife were the invited guests. We had what is called here a splendid dinner—Ham, Eggs, Oyster pie, Roast Beef and potatoes, peach tarts and cup custards. Everything passed off nicely and Dr. Dudley said he enjoyed having them which he is seldom known to say; he generally anathematizes visitors in about the same language that father does—March 6th, I have just received today a nice cooking stove like the one Mary Shepherd has, it was a present from Sallie Ingham and I appreciate it highly as I have had a very smoky one for a great while. It will belong to me and when the Army moves I can have it stored at the Sanitary Com in Washington and they will have it sent to any point for me. It is burning beautifully now, the pipe goes right through the canvas and draws like a steamboat.

I have received all the papers right along both thine and William's. I see William spoken of in connection with the legislature. Kilpatrick has taken the cavalry and gone somewhere towards Richmond. Meade I see is to be court martialed for the retreat from Gettysburg. U. S. Grant they are going to spoil before he gets through his career. I detest War and officers, if you could know of the drunkedness and bearing of our Major generals down here you would feel indeed disgusted with military affairs. Men who have been in the Army for nearly two years are almost demented to go home. Nothing exceeds the loneliness of a sunny Sunday in camp. Dr. Miller of the 12 N. J. improves on acquaintance. Dr. Dudley has not been well for some time and is not near as pleasant

58

as when he is well. This letter is what I call long drawn out, there is nothing new to say so I will close with much love to all the family. Tell father *he must* plant some trees on Bobby's lot for I am going to build a log house certain, as soon as I get home— They are so very comfortable.

From thy daugher

CORNELIA HANCOCK

I write thee while I am keeping score for our doctors while they play cards; that is the only amusement they have here and at night I sometimes get lonesome and go over and sit with them.

3rd Div. 2nd Corps Hospt., Brandy
Sta. Va., March 5th, 1864.

MY DEAR SISTER

THERE are days of great rejoicing in camp that come to us once in a while, but the greatest ones we ever know is when boxes are received or letters. Today therefore has been a big day with me. My box came, things all, especially Dr. Dudley's, very satisfactory. If I had received my shoes on a rainy day I should have been mad and I fear I shall be now when a wet day comes but today has been splendid and my feet were just on the ground. I was going to have company to dinner, wanted to dress up, so thee may see I was all ready for them. Dr. Dudley wishes me to state his great indebtedness to thee and say if it is ever in his power to do thee a favor he certainly will do it. He was astounded at the dispatch with which I received them. He says he intends to write his people that he has some friends if they have all deserted him. In addition to the box I received thy letter.

The rumors about the army you hear much more about than we do here. The sixth Corps I believe has been over the Rapidan and Kilpatrick and the Cavalry have been somewhere, but nothing can disturb the equanimity of "old soldiers" and therefore no account is made of moving unless we have orders so to do ourselves. Dr.

59

Dudley is not *pro*-slavery, that is he does not wish for slavery to exist but he thinks nothing of the black man himself, he thinks they are nobody and ought never to be anybody. I always speak my mind and when that is done my duty is done and I do try not to take other people's sins upon me any more than I can help. He is not enlightened at all upon politics. He has always been a hard student, is a graduate of Yale College, entered the army as a private and has had very little opportunity to know much of politics. He is a very shrewd man and ought to know better than he talks. Time may work wonders with him. He seemed to be so overcome with gratitude for the things. I told him he could do well by me and that would recompense you as well as doing for you! He thinks he certainly will do that and I certainly cannot complain of him in regard to any matter. He is a satisfactory man, willing to listen to suggestions and profit by them if good ones. I have my way in everything which thee may know I enjoy after the life I led in Washington. He always says to any mooted question, "Just as Miss Hancock says." I have one man detailed to work for me and one old man that has taken it up of his own accord and Dr. says I can have both if I want. This old man is a jack of all trades; on the walls of my log house he has made a wreathe of evergreens and put white paper for a background and in the middle is a blue club with my medal festooned in the center of that, all together it is a pretty thing. He has also made me a lounge that I defy any upholsterer to beat for shape and comfort, the back and arms are all stuffed, I am sitting on it now. If thee had only sent him a box of tacks thee would have made him happy. He builds my fire in the morning, keeps it hot all day, does everything. I live just like a queen on her throne. I am willing to work for the contrabands whenever I am not in a field Hospital, shall always give my voice to advocate their cause. But I know I am calculated to do much in a field hospital and shall be there whenever there is a chance.

I have no fault to find with thy letter writing. Try to get Corps spelled right on the outside of thy next letter though. I received

Lizzie's letter and will answer. I would wonderfully like to see the children. The desire to see your home and friends no one knows better than the component parts of the Army of Potomac. That cry goes up from morning until night, "I want to go home, if I could only get a furlough—"

from thy sister

CORNELIA HANCOCK

3rd Div. 2nd Corps Hospt. Brandy, Va.
March 12th, 1864.

MY DEAR SISTER

Do not worry about the army. They do not intend to go to Richmond and while the ale and whiskey holds out all the officers don't care, and the privates know it is a great ways farther than they wish to *march*. We don't want to *go* anywhere, just be let alone and be allowed to keep our men comfortable.

Dr. Dudley has applied for ten days leave of absence which he will get as he has never been absent except when wounded. Dr. Dwinelle and Mrs. start next Wednesday and will stop one day at the Continental Hotel, Phila. Dr. Dudley talks some of going on with them to New Haven. So you may see him. Dr. Dwinelle will of course come to see you, and if there is any politeness such as taking them round in the carriage I hope you will do it for my sake as they are very strong friends of mine. I write this tonight that you may be on the lookout for them.

I have wasted this evening nursing a dog and keeping score for Dr. Miller and Dr. Dudley to play cards; there is much time wasted in the Army; if it was not for wasting my time I would learn to play cards. Sunday evening—here is another evening almost squandered. I get so tired of the wan faces, and "please to give me a lemon," the pots, kettles and pans, that about sundown I go into the Doctors Quarters and they order their supper, then sit round a bright open fire and converse for an hour. Tonight a religious fit

61

seized them, they sent for a bible and we had about six chapters read and explained. Dr. Dudley had had more religious training than either of the other party. . . .

3rd Div. 2nd Corps Hospt.
Brandy Sta., Va., March 16, 1864.

MY DEAR SARAH

I RECEIVED thy letter two evenings ago. I was lying upon my sofa fast asleep when a second Div. ambulance driver brought it to me. All in the encampment know me and anyone who can hunt up a letter seems delighted with an excuse to bring it to me. Dr. Dwinelle and wife started for the north this morning. It made me feel quite homesick. Dr. Dudley starts tomorrow on a ten days leave, he goes to New Haven, expects to stop in Phila. and go to the Doctor's. We are mending up his trunk, cleaning his things generally previous to his departure. The steward and I are going to take charge of the hospt. while he is gone. We cannot be boss when *he* is here and we will see if we cannot work Dr. Miller so he will be merely a *nominal* surgeon-in-charge! I did receive the box of pads with 1 dozen eggs and one pound of butter. I shall acknowledge the receipt of it to the president of the society soon. I am going to have rice pudding for dinner, Roast beef and onions, toast and tea, eggs when ordered. We live well here almost all the time. I do not suppose there is a trip thee could take that would give thee more pleasure, the scenery is beautiful; what magnificent residences will rear their heads in these hills after the sounds of war cease! I do not remember whether I told you of my visit to Col. Thomas' house. It is a pile of ruins, even the dungeons where he kept his slaves are level with the ground. All his papers lie scattered round. I picked up a few the date of which were the most ancient that I could find.

I have also a few flowers that were picked from St. Helena Island in S. C., picked by Dr. Dudley's sister; he set no store by them so I said I would send them to thee. We have lots of daffodils nearly ready to bloom. As soon as they do I will send thee one. I have made my puddings and they are in Sallie Ingham's stove; it works to a charm. It is a very windy day, Paddy's I believe. Mrs. Dwinelle is 37 years old today. I dressed myself in my best dress and went to the steward and got a piece of Red flannel about two yds. in length that had some black bars through it, wore it for a scarf and went to the Dwinelle's to spend the evening. She was out so I went into the Doctor's tent and my being dressed seemed to have great effect upon them. We have but two chairs, and I was proferred one of them. You, I have no doubt, think I speak much of myself and the Doctors. There is nothing else to speak of except the sick men and anything you wish to know of them I can tell you, for I know nearly all that goes on in this hospital.

I am going to the third Corps to see Mrs. Husbands with Dr. Aiken. He is Surg-in-charge of 2nd Div. Hospt. He has asked me to go many places with him, but never struck a fortunate invite until this one. She is an old lady I met at Gettysburg and one I admire very much. The N. Jersey Brigade is in that Corps, more from N. J. there than any place in the army. Do you ever hear anything of the 2 N. J. Cor.? I have never heard a syllable from them since they went down the Tennessee river. I feel that their fate is nearly sealed, as they are detailed to fight Guerrillas. Yesterday a man was brought in all mashed up, a heavy wagon ran right over his leg. His leg was amputated and in an hour after I saw one of the Drs. cut it up into three pieces for the sake of practice. One can get used to anything. One of my favorite resorts is our dead house, some such fine looking men die. Sometimes Dr. Dudley embalms them and keeps them quite a while just to look at. Men are put into neat coffins and buried very decently from this hospital.

My dresses are commencing to tear. I wish I had some of Uncle Williams apples— All boxes are opened that come to the army now. My fire is nearly out. It is cold tonight, so I must go to bed.

From thy attached Aunt,

"MISS HANCOCK"

63

3rd Div. 2nd Corps Hospital
Near Brandy Sta., Va., March 20, 1864.

MY DEAR SISTER

I RECEIVED thy letter this evening apprising me of the coming of the box. I shall not concern about it as Capt. Madison is at Gen. Hays Head Qrs. and he dispatches them to me as soon as they arrive. Mother's came through straight as a die. I wish thee had delayed writing one more day and may be Doctor Dudley's visit might have been described. Mrs. Dwinelle did not favor stopping in Phila. I suppose she carried the day and went right through to New Haven. If so, Doctor Dwinelle will stop on his return. Doctor Dudley started a day later, said he should go direct to Phila. But when people travel for pleasure, their movements are very uncertain.

I do not wish you to exert yourselves to send me anything more as our surgeons are so good about using the hospital fund that I do not believe we shall want long for anything. There is a system about all they do and there is not that several days interim of starvation like used to be experienced at Gettysburg. I am like Miss Rebecca Thompson. I feel it is a blessed privilege we are giving the people, to contribute to the comfort of our wounded men; but all do not feel it so. Tonight will be the last on earth for one of our wounded men. He was one day a soldier, then he was shot at Morton's Ford and has been suffering ever since from a wound in the knee joint. It is blowing very hard tonight. Billy (colored) is building up a big fire. He acts just like magic upon it. We have with us tonight Maj. Hutchins, paymaster for our Division. He has paid all our sick and wounded this evening. We have an extra guard on. There was a very interesting spectacle seeing the men come in to be paid hobbling along on crutches and canes; most of them received $50. Some fine looking young men—it seemed much like a pittance to me, considering their wounds. They all seemed pleased, are going to bed praising Dr. F. A. Dudley for securing the paymaster to come to the hospt. He is wide awake and attends to their interest in many ways they never had before. Now he has put in for furloughs and I

64

guess he will get his men off before the 2nd Division does although they have been longer at it. The rats have gnawed my two hoods so they cannot be worn. I am wearing now a piece of red flannel doubled, plaited behind with black strings. It looks very fantastic and is tolerably comfortable. I do not want another as I shall soon need a hat. There are many rumors about moving, it would not be strange that if by the time Dr. Dudley's leave expires he would find this camp a ruins and the army back upon Centreville. Gen. Grant has assumed the reigns of government and no doubt he will make some change. The 11 & 12 Army Corps have been ordered back to the Army of the Potomac, I believe, and it is supposed the 2nd Corps will go somewhere. But sufficient unto the day is the evil thereof and I am not concerned. There was heavy artillery firing at Corps Head Qrs. yesterday. It sounded awfully but it was practice only. But we never know when we hear it what it is. I feel very much obliged for the shoes, breastpin, and other articles forthcoming. I was out of stamps but the Christian Commission gave me 12 today, they are very kind to me; copy the inscription upon my medal every day. It hangs upon the wall of my house in a blue trefoil surrounded with a wreathe of evergreens. It is always shown to all the Generals that come. Between thee and me and the gatepost, that medal has done much for me in this hospital, that, and my pass from the Sec. of War. Dr. Dudley was almost forced to sign the request that brought me here, and had I been any ordinarily recommended person I do not believe I would have fared as well as I have. He is an ambitious man and I think feels that I add to the reputation of the hospital and for that reason blows my horn. I may do him injustice, but I think not. He is good to the wounded, prompt in every action, a general favorite in his regt. and is polite to me and that is enough and more than you generally find in men in the army. Dr. Miller is a real pleasant man. And all things *so far* work harmoniously. I ought to wait until I receive the box to mail this letter but I do not like to have letters lying round so shall seal it up. The paymaster is concerned about my pay and if he chooses to pay me I shall receive it

65

without hesitation, he has just been in my shanty, seems quite struck —no doubt with my flannel bonnet.

From thy sister

CORNELIA

3rd Div. 2nd Corps Hospital
Near Brandy Sta., Va., March 20, 1864.

MY DEAR MOTHER

You have no idea what a sameness seems to pervade your place regarded from my standpoint. The same time of year seems to bring round the same events precisely. I believe I see about the best times, take it all in all, of any of the family. They sent me word the Provost Martial had some papers for me, of what nature I do not know. It always scares me when any military authority summons me. I cannot get used to the tyrannical sway of men in authority, it may be merely something relative to a box. I really have nothing to fear, for before God and man I could testify that no woman has served the Army of the Potomac with any more self denial or faithfulness than I have. But our old cook says that God Almighty does not reign in the A. P., that *it* is under military rule, and such seems to be the case. Dr. Dudley has gone north on a furlough, he expects to go to the Doctor's while he is in Phila. He has no friends in the North at all, went to New Haven to put his money into some safe shape. *Sunday:* I have just finished giving out dinner, mashed potatoes, roast beef, tomatoes, toast, tea and raspberry pie. The Christian Commission have made their daily round, copied the inscription upon my medal, left me plenty of postage stamps, promised to bring much the next time they come. My letters carry very well I think, considering the number of hands they pass through. The eggs carried all right and the pads have healed many a bed sore. Think how much more comfortable to lay a wounded thigh upon than sticks and leaves, which their beds are filled with. I thought the box came very direct. It is all right to cooperate with the Sanitary but I

66

should reserve the privilege of sending boxes to individuals; pads I always want, all edibles I like to have; but *clothing*, the Sanitary is the proper channel for.

I am glad the contrabands have some friends among you. I do not swear *much* yet. If Sallie would only get well and you all keep alive until I get home I shall be very thankful. I never realized what valuable acquisitions relations were as since I have been in the army. Sallie's stove is a treasure, it never smokes even when the wind blows.

I shall just suit father when I get home. I know how to boil and bake beans and like them extremely well. I am not joking. I intend to build that log house, they are as comfortable as they can be. That ingrain carpet I should have embalmed for the good it has done.

The paymaster has come and I hear great rejoicing among the patients. I do not suppose he has brought any for me and I do not need it as I have plenty yet.

I just received a letter from Ellen saying they had despatched $10. worth of goods to me. I suppose it will be forthcoming soon. Capt. Madison is Brigade Provost Martial and he generally sends my boxes right to me without any trouble.

This summers campaign is very much dreaded by all belonging to the A. of P. I hope thee will not learn to sneeze as loud as grandmother did, thee may ape her in almost everything but that. I am glad there is a prospect of a garden but I think it is well for father to oppose it.

from thy affectionate daughter
CORNELIA HANCOCK

3rd Div. 2 Corps Hospital
March 25, 1864.

MY DEAR SISTER

I AM sorry Mrs. Dwinelle made so short stay as she is a lady I admire much. Dr. Dudley was not very well when he left. Thee would not think him too young for his position if thee could see him perform here and know how we miss him now he is gone. I think if he had known how things would have been he would not have left. Compare him with the *old* doctors thee would soon make a choice in his favor. I did not doubt thee would let his pro-slavery proclivities bias thy opinion of him. Age will bring him out of many of his opinions. I wish you had seen him in the clothes he left here in, they show the service he has rendered. His clothes were ordered in Phila. and I suppose boy like he jumped right in them. The old ones, he has grown about one inch out of since they were made, and in them he looks more natural to us. It is wrong in my way of thinking not to allow freedom of speech and thought *even* on the slavery question. I would be much better pleased if both our Doctors were abolitionists, but still I think they have a perfect right *not* to be, and allow them the privilege they take. Dr. Miller is worse than Dudley and still I like him very much; they have many very good qualities and for them I like them. If it was to come to the pinch of a suffering contraband they would work to help them and that is more than many clamoring abolitionists would do. Dr. Dudley amputated the limb of a poor fellow only a week ago and he concerned about him until he died. That is the only ridiculous part of thy character. Holding abolitionism in the van of all other spiritual qualifications. To like a negro and to do him justice does not exercise all the parts of a Christian's character. To be able to love a white man *equally* well with the black is my kind of humanity. Thee speaks of living with Dr. Dudley. I never knew it in camp to be more emphatically so than here. Since Dudley has been gone it seems almost to me as if Dr. Miller was afraid to stay alone. All day I work, and he saunters round and lies on the sofa in my kitchen. When evening comes we both go to their house and do almost anything to kill time, play cards, chess, eat oysters, &c. Mr. Holbrook, Sanitary Com. agent is here this evening, playing with Dr. Miller. I am writing. We have a bright fire on the hearth, a dog lying round and much more stillness and quiet than when Dr. Dudley is here. Neither doctors have been out to spend but one evening since I have been here. I think that creditable to all

68

parties. Sunday we look for Dudley back and there is not a patient or an attendant but what will be glad to see him. On Wednesday we received orders to send all the sick and wounded to Washington, along with the order came a snow storm, along with the snow storm came an orderly countermanding the previous order, along with him came a splendid morning, along with it, came another orderly ordering to move on Thursday; and at 8 o'clock we had them all loaded and on stretchers, and proceeded with the long train from the three hospitals to Brandy station. There the platform was strewed full of helpless men wounded at Morton's Ford. How like Gettysburg it seemed to me. I had all our worst cases put in a pile, took a whiskey bottle, and sat down and helped the poor souls to live while they were loaded. Two mortal hours we sat in the sun and heard the locomotive hiss, the cars back and go ahead, then back, etc., etc., etc., just what always happens at depots. One of our nice wounded wanted to give me some greenbacks right in the hubbub. There were two women who stay at the station with hot tea, etc. They supplied all hands and retired. There I sat, I suppose five hundred men staring at me, but Dr. Miller and our own steward and hospital boys were with me and I did not care. By dint of great perseverance a hospital car was provided for the worst cases and I went in and saw them lying comfortably upon the stretchers, saw the cars trudge off with their groaning load, and think I to myself, the idea of making a *business* of *maiming men* is not one worthy of a civilized nation. By the time I got home over the corduroy had a headache of the first water, went to bed and there could lay, as my occupation is nearly gone now. Those low diet men have gone away. I am, however, all right today, have washed my blue sacque, mended my dress and am endeavoring to make myself look more respectable on poor capital. We shall soon fill up from the Regt. Hospitals if a move is not made. If so I shall do something sensible I hope. If the hospital organization is kept up the calculation is for me to move with it. If an ambulance is detailed to carry Mrs. Lee I will go with her. I am no ways anxious about the future, shall do nothing rash or romantic you may rest assured.

69

Shall abide much by Dr. Dwinelle's advice and he has always led me a right. I should be very glad to make a visit home before the summer campaigne. We know nothing an hour ahead down here so I can give you very little satisfaction. But I think that as I have made a successful campaigne of nearly 9 months you ought to confide in my judgment of what is best for me to do. I think you do generally but thy and mother's letters seem as if you might be a little restive at present. Mother says the prevailing opinion in Salem is I should have a female companion to sleep in my house. My house is in a thickly settled neighborhood, two doors of which fasten securely, the corporal of the guard lives in the next house to mine, the sentinel walks the beat at the side of my house. I feel more secure than in your third story, for *there* I am afraid sometime. Here I am not at all. I always lie down in security. I am asleep as soon as I touch the bed, so do rest easy. It is raining right hard tonight, would thee think I would be making caramels here? But true it is. Holbrook, Dr. Miller and myself made some; right good it is too. If Grant reviews the army I am going. I wish I had a riding dress here. I would go on horseback as it makes my head ache to ride over the corduroy. Dr. Maull, division surg. of the 3rd Division, asked me to come over to Head Qrs. he wanted I should. It seems as if I had got in with a better run of Doctors than were at Gettysburg. I think they felt that probably they would have another battle then and took their best away. Anyhow I have met with some good and efficient ones here this winter. I am sorry to hear of any conviction on the subject of spiritualism, but everybody has a right to their opinions, especially their religious ones. I do not believe in it, *emphatically*. I could have told Grandmother Nicholson would have approved my course without consulting any *oracles*. I received thy last letter, also the box in good order, not 1/2 doz. eggs were broken. I was very much obliged for it, had no butter when it came. The breast pin I have broken already. The tacks were well thought of; were not the apples from William's? I am sure anyone might call this a spicy letter. I hope it will meet with

70

approbation and if not I will write soon again in a different strain. Was D. at home while my friends were there.

from thy affectionate sister

CORNELIA HANCOCK

3rd Div. 2 Corps Hosp.
March 27th, 1864.

MY DEAR MOTHER

I RECEIVED a short letter from thee last night. Before this thee has no doubt received my last. Has Joanna received a letter acknowledging the receipt of the box of pads? We have sent all our wounded and bad sick to Washington. I followed them to the depot and saw them loaded into the car. It was a Gettysburg over again. By the time I arrived back at my house over the corduroy roads my head ached and I went to bed which I could do as all but four of the men I take care of were gone. Our hospital will soon fill up with sick unless they move. Then what will become of us is unknown. Ellen is fretting for fear I shall go on a march. My only answer to all such worriments is you ought to have confidence enough in my judgment to think I will do the best thing. After campaigning successfully for 9 months I ought to have some experience. In regard to Salem people thinking I ought to have a woman to sleep with me, I am much better guarded than the lone widows and maids at Isabelle's. Another woman is not needed nor would be allowed here. Mrs. Lee is within sending distance if I was sick, so calm all your fears. I go to sleep just as quick as I touch the bed, am used to being alone, like it, and never feel lonely and would not sleep with Mrs. Lee if I could. I am sorry you have any distress on my account, but I cannot help you any and I assure you it is all unnecessary. Dr. Dudley we expect back tomorrow that will be a day of rejoicing here, he has been gone 10 days and I am tired of hearing the men wishing him back. He called to see Ellen while he was in Phila. She said she could not help letting his

71

sins trouble her—his not being an abolitionist. I think that very foolish. I do not think the salvation of one's soul depends upon your being an abolitionist. Dr. Dudley does his duty well as a soldier and has done more towards crushing this rebellion than some of the ranting abolitionists.

Everybody has gone from the hospital, steward, asst. steward, some nurses and nearly all the patients; it is very lonesome indeed. Dr. Aiken, one of my especial friends, is quite sick. I have been taking care of him. He is a good man and has worked himself down sick.

Sunday morning—our steward has returned quite drunk and things have not got straightened yet, quite. Liquor I am so down upon. They cannot get it here but he went to Washington and has not recovered himself yet. He has just been in my house, says he is all right for duty now. I hope so. My house is not swept up yet. I suppose you are about getting off to Meeting.

Sarah S—— wrote me a letter expressive of great concern from my "way of living." I wrote her a letter that she will not forget soon. They cannot expect everyone to be satisfied to live in as small a circle as themselves in these days of great events. She expresses it as the great concern of the whole family and her approaching sickness made her bold to express it.

The men say they would like to have one of Father's shad. I am well, comfortable and happy, and after our men get sober around here all things will be right again.

from thy daughter
CORNELIA HANCOCK

We are now mixed up with third Corps. I do not know how we shall be effected by it in the end. U. S. Grant is raising many new arrangements hereabouts.

Hospt—March 30th, 1864.

DEAR DOCTOR [1]

I RECEIVED a letter from thee dated Feb. 15. I have kept it in my un-

---

[1] Her brother-in-law, Dr. Child.

72

answered box all this time. But have thought I had to write so continually about little matters to Ellen that probably you heard from me full as often as you cared to.

Our third Division is played out by command of Lieut. Gen. U. S. Grant. I believe thee always held with the *second* Division. Much of the fighting that the second Corps participated in was done by the *third*. When the artillery practice it makes me feel just as the first week at Gettysburg, it is awful; sometimes it booms forth for a whole day and we know not whether it is a battle or not. I do not know whether I want to see a battle or not. I suppose my seeing it would make it no worse, but it is terrible. The soldiers dread very much this summer's campaign but always speak with more feeling of the *marching* than the fighting. Dr. Dwinelle has not returned yet from his leave. I wish he would. I like him very much. His position is not much of a one though when the surgeons in charge of the *Divisions* attend well to *their* business. He is not needed here at all now. A wounded man is a sad sight but saddest yet are the sights in our hospital now, cases of Chronic Diarrhea, men emaciated to a skeleton and blacker than a mulatto. Oh! how awful it is, they are very much more trouble, too, to care for than wounded; they are full of notions, and have no appetite whatever.

Our hospital keeps full most of the time. Home furloughs, and the expiration of their term of service are the themes talked upon by the soldiers, most of them now have not seen civilization for 2 years. Ambulance driver Jeff has re-enlisted. I was surprised at that but the very ones who clamor most loudly against their situation you find first to re-enlist.

The butter and eggs came very opportunely as we were just out. Mrs. Lee is still flourishing. She talks and cooks as much as ever. Dr. Aiken thinks she is the best woman he ever saw in a hospital and Dr. Dudley says he would not have her in *his* hospital 24 hours. So you see all tastes are not alike. Mrs. Lee would never get along with Dudley in this world. I will say for her I do think she is one of the best women, all things considered, I ever did see. Dr. Aiken is a great

73

friend of mine, too, and offers me to stay if he has charge, but I know I had better take the First alone than *part* of the Second with Mrs. Lee.

There is nothing new to relate except the consolidating of the army and that you will see in the papers.

from thy affectionate sister

C. HANCOCK

Hospt., March 30th, 1864.

MY DEAR SISTER

I GAVE a full description of the wounded getting off in my last letter. I felt at first it would be impossible to move them until Dr. Dudley was here but I think it was done quite well and much more quietly than if he had been here. I do not wish to go into a general hospital in Washington. I shall come home as soon as I leave here. We are in a most unsettled state here at present. The third Division is *annihilated* from the face of the earth and I suppose Dr. Dudley will be relieved here and go to his Regt. [the 14th Connecticut] in about a week. But we know nothing until Dr. Dougherty, Corps director, gets home, so it is not worth while for me to undertake to say. Our Division is broken up and goes part in the Second and part in the First. The third Brigade composed of 111 N. Y. 126. 135 N. Y. go into the First and to them I am very much attached and as Mrs. Lee reigns supreme in the 2nd Division, I shall go over there and work until moving time comes. Dr. Dudley despises the Second Division, says he would rather I would go into a colored soldiers hospital than be under the second Division doctors. He is in the right of that, as with the exception of Dr. Aiken, I never admired anyone attached to it. Dr. Aiken has offered me to remain just as I am and take two rows of tents in second Div. But if I stay I shall go to first Div. Dr. Dudley says he will see everything moved and give me everything that he bought for my house to carry into first Div. He says he is going to tear his *own* house down when he leaves and carry everything valu-

74

able with him to his Regt. He is perfectly disconsolate about the death of the Third Division, they have to wear the *white* trefoil now. He says if I will promise to wear the Blue trefoil he will buy me a handsome one. *They* are obliged to change. I am not. The steward of our Division goes to the 1st Division. Therefore, wants red. In thy next letter I want thee to send me a piece of bright red velvet about two inches square. Buy it if thee has none. The Doctor gave him his old blue one with a gold edge and the middle has to be changed. Do not forget it. Claret color (bright), crimson I guess I mean.

Dr. Dudley is to be relieved from duty here tomorrow and goes to his Regt. I am very sorry. I always look out expecting things to be uncomfortable in camp life but had almost made up my mind that this campaign was to be an entire success. Could not see any trouble ahead as he always anticipated events and kept things righted up. There is not a dissenting voice of the one cry that all are sorry to have him leave, he did more for the men than feed and clothe them, he discharged them and furloughed with more facility than any one I ever saw handle red tape. His Regt. is about six miles from here and we shall not see him very often. The Surg. of the First Division is a nice man. I like him very well, but not any better than Dudley. Dr. Aiken promises very fair that if I will stay where I am I can care for two rows of tents and have everything I want, but he thinks well of Mrs. Lee and I think she can get along with the whole.—One of the men gave me a bible today they picked up on the Battlefield of Gettysburg. I will try to keep it. I have a silver quarter, a button from the coat Dudley wore when he was wounded, and various other trophies that if I get them home I shall try to take care of.

April 2nd—I have not finished this letter for the reason I could give no settled news and if thee was here tonight thee would think it was far from being settled yet. Orders however, have been issued that every well person, officers and all, report to their respective Regt. without delay and all sick be sent to either first or second Division. Dr. Aiken took charge of all pertaining to the old third Division today, ordered our cookhouse down, my dominions he

75

wanted should stay undisturbed and me to do for the ones I had done for just the same; but thinking it will operate better in the end I threw up my commission with the rest. As soon as Dr. Potter heard I would not stay under second Division rule he wants I should come to his Division, so Dr. Dudley and he are building me a house, in their *minds*, to be put up tomorrow. I expect they will take my present one to pieces and turn it in over there. Dr. Dudley says that out on the front they are all as drunk as they can be over the changes in the Division, that about 1/4 of the officers of the third Corps are under arrest for disobedience of orders. He came back home, said there was no possibility of keeping sober there. He has been carrying on almost like a mad man here this evening; most of the men who work round the hospital are drunk, and to a raw hand in camp it might seem a rough way of living, but nothing could happen to surprise *me* much. Dr. Maull, surg. of the 1st Del. Rgt. a great friend of mine, sent me his compliments and says I had better come over to the front and see the indignation at the death of the 3rd Division there. It certainly is sorrowful to me as I began to know all the officers from Gen. Hays down. Now they are all scattered. Today my gum shoes and leggins have been in requisition; it has been sleeting and snowing here and very disagreeable. Our steward fell from his horse going to Corps. Head Qrs. and sprained his foot and is laid up. In a few words, the once *most flourishing* Division of the Corps has gone completely to smash. I will write again in a few days. You may direct my letters 2nd Corps Hospital near Brandy Sta. I am known at Corps Head Qrs. and I do not know what Doctor to have them directed to yet. When I am installed in the 1st Division I shall occupy Miss Holstein's proper place. She is sick I believe. I hope after a battle Dr. Maull will have charge of the hospt. and he will want me instead of Mrs. Lee. Dr. Dudley I do not think will ever accept the appointment again, he did not want it at this time. I would like Dr. Maull full as well. He is an older man and very much of a gentleman. Dudley did first rate until the 3rd Div. death, since that he has done nothing but make a general row. He has had no authority to do

76

anything else. I never saw as much life in the men in the army before. It is really refreshing. The general tenor of the men is gaping and yawning, but words and anathemas have fairly poured from them since the consolidation has commenced. I wish I was like Mrs. Lee, did not think about anything but my biscuit, yeast, etc. She is delighted to have my Division to cook for, the more work she has to do the better she feels. We have 66 sick men after all we sent to Washington.

U. S. Grant is creating great activity in the army now; he is bringing out the heavy artillery men who have been lying round Washington, arming them with muskets and bringing them to the front. That gratifies the inmost souls of these veterans here; a perfect sea of heads come up from Brandy Sta. every day. One Regt. 2400 strong, went up to Corps Head Qrs. and in an hour's time eighteen were sent here sick. It is very exposing for them; there are no quarters for them and it is very bad weather. Nobody knows what soldiering is until they try it. It will do in dry weather, but to have *water* dripping over you 23 hours out of 24 is not as pleasant as one might suppose, as I can testify from experience.

from thy affectionate sister

CORNELIA HANCOCK

somewhere in the Army of the Potomac
satisfied with her lot.

I find in the confusion of affairs this letter has not been mailed. My house has been taken to pieces and carried into the 1st Division. I am occupying temporarily a nice tent formerly Dr. Rowland's, Asst. Surg. here. It is as comfortable as possible and a splendid open fire. Dr. Potter lives in style, I tell thee, his wife was here all winter and they have silver forks and spoons and set a table full as nice as yours. I eat my dinner and tea with Dr. Potter and Dr. Rowland. Dr. Dudley is a guest here until he settles his accts. and then he goes to his Regt. in Stony Mt. close to the Rebs. I believe I shall like it even better

77

here than in third Division. Sarah Sinnickson has a daughter. I wish some of my friends could *be here nights*. The Salem people have got up a perfect panic about the "way" I live. I wish they could know the exact state of things, they would calm their fears. I think thee will have to buy me a domestic Gingham dress and trim it with braid some way so it will be decent. I go in such good society and still have to work, thus I will have to combine the ornamental with the beautiful. I mean by domestic gingham such as is as stout as bed ticking; my shoes are all worn out, what will I do? You had better have me a leather pair made. I have but one presentable suit, that is the blue, except my best dress. The corduroy walks are bordered with cedar brush on either side and that has worn threadbare two breadths of my dress.

Somewhere in the Army of the Potomac
April 6, 1864.

MY DEAR MOTHER

IF it is any satisfaction to people to receive letters from me it certainly is very little effort for me to write them. I write so much that I even fancy my handwriting is improving. I hope the war and pestilence thee speaks of stalking through the land will have the effect to so purify our souls that we may have a good time in the World to come, for sure it is I do not wish to spend more than one life in the hospital.

We have a splendid day which we are enjoying extremely. There has been such a long continued rain storm. It almost seemed to me as if I could not bear to hear the pattering on the tent cloth any longer; the mud on the roads is about four feet deep and all the army can do it cannot move for some time yet. Our hospitals are full up. The recruits are brought down so fast that there is not shelter enough to keep them from the weather. The consequence is they fall sick immediately and are carried here. I am quite busy, we have very sick men. Dr. Dudley is relieved here and has gone to his Regt. which is stationed on the extreme front. I expected to come home when

78

the hospt. was broken up but Dr. Potter, surg-in-charge of the first Division, found it out and wanted I should stay in his hospital, so they took my house down bodily and are now putting it up over here. I occupy meanwhile a hospital tent with a nice floor in it with an open fire. I believe I like a tent as well as a house except in the night it is not as private. Lieut. Fogg, who was detailed at Gen. Hays Head Quarters, was home on leave of absence when the third Division was broken up and when he came back he did not find as much as a tin cup of his things. I am the refuge of everyone who knows me, and I gave him two cups and two spoons. He is a very nice young man. He is only across the corduroy from us now and he comes over frequently. Dr. Dudley says I would take care of a Jersey man and let all from other states go to the d——l if I could not do both. That I think an unfair speech, for I know I have taken care of him well. The last few days he staid round, I had all his meals to get. He would not eat the food belonging to the second Division. If he does not miss the comforts he has enjoyed this winter, now he is way out at the front I shall be mistaken. I like Dr. Potter very well, he is much more refined and gentlemanly in his deportment than Dudley, but I do not think his hospital has quite as much *vim* about it as our old one.

Mrs. Husbands, Miss Gilson, and Mrs. McRay, three ladies who have been round in the third Corps and much at Army Head Qrs. have had their orders to leave. I have rec'd none yet; so much for not being known. I have never been to the front yet; have never left the hospital grounds but twice since I first came. It is no place for ladies in the *Regt.* but it is just like home to me in these *hospitals*. We know each other so well; everybody has his own house and we live just as in a little village of huts. I am very much grieved that Gen. Grant should deem it necessary to break up the third Division as I had got to be well known there and got on first rate. Now I shall have a new set soon to learn. Genl. Barlow was here this morning. He is Division general. I should not think to look at him he was 25 years old. He asked Dr. Potter who I was and by what authority I was there, whether I did any good? He evidently is pretty acute in his observa-

79

tion, there was not a spot in the hospital that he did not look into. He was wounded at Antietam; at Gettysburg did several daring feats such as capturing flags, etc. He is young to have such responsibility, but Dr. Dudley has cured me of thinking *age* is necessary to have charge here.—He commanded his *hospital* and they say Genl. Barlow commands his *Division*.

1st Div. 2nd Corps Hospt.
April 12th, 1864.

MY DEAR MOTHER

WE have been stormed almost out and the bridges all floated away and tonight is the first mail we have received for some time—most faithful thing, and harbinger of more joy than any thing on earth I believe. Thy letter bore date of April 5th. I think it very unkind of thee to wish me to come home to a pestilence. It is fearfully unhealthy for *new* recruits here, but old soldiers seem to weather it well. Measles is the prevailing disease.

The Salem people's concern has no effect upon me whatever. You cannot know *how* we live here unless you could be here. I cannot explain, but there is so much distinction in different rank, and I rank about as high as anything around. No soldier would be allowed to come into my house without knocking even in the day time and at night they could not get in without sawing out the logs. There is no danger from any thing in the army, except an *unsophisticated* individual might possibly have their affections trifled. But as I have long since found I had no affections to be trifled with, I am the very one to be here. I believe I wrote thee a letter telling thee of my moving to the first Division hospital. My house is all done again and I have an open fire of my own now. I have my stove up in an adjoining shanty, and my front room now has blankets for carpet, two tables two chairs and is a regular army parlor. No one could be more comfortably situated than I am tonight. I have been busy all day doing something for our very sick men, have just come into my house, found my fire all blazing, my candle lighted and everything

80

as cheerful as possible. There is nothing the men would not do to enhance my comfort—to build me a house twice is a proof.

Shall plant my seeds but not with faith I shall see them grow while I stay here; though I did not expect to see my hyacinths and daffodils and they have done beautifully; nothing is more gloriously uncertain than military affairs. My tent is next to Dr. Potter's, they have the whole assemblage of Surgeons, Aiken, Dwinelle, Rowland, &c. in to night playing cards. It is just as much a habit to play cards immediately after getting together as it is to ask each other to take a seat. I can hear their conversation, they wanted I should stay in but I wanted to write this letter. I will never say so much against any class of men as I did against surgeons until I have seen them all. The ones I have met this winter have so faithfully performed their duty I think them very necessary to the well being of the army. Dr. Dudley does business more the way I like to see business done than any of the rest but he is no better man than Dr. Aiken or Dr. Potter. Thee makes a comment that he looks as if he might easily be ruled. I wish thee had seen people try to rule him as often as I have and thee would change thy mind. He is too young looking in that picture and too thin. It was taken after he was wounded. Dr. Aiken is no fool and has many good traits but he never could govern men like Dudley; they hate Miller and would walk on their heads to accomodate Dudley. Dr. Dudley has gone to his Regt. and has never been back to see us since he left.

Dr. Rowland, Asst. Surg. in this hospital, has a flute and plays at the proper time and not very long, just like father. He is a widower, has been eleven years. He is the most proper intelligent, rich, and agreeable man one would find in a day's ride. The orders are published that every *citizen* must leave the army the 16 of this month. Every order culminates on that date. Every person found within the lines after that date is to be put to *hard labor*. That would be no more punishment than is inflicted upon me every day. I think I shall stay around this hospital, orders or no orders, until they stop bringing in 7 or eight sick per day. When they march I would like to go home.

I shall have to have everything very much to my liking to induce me to make a march. But it would not be much change in reality for the same men are in charge and the only difference would be we would be in ambulances instead of tents. In fact, a person after they have been in this wilderness as long as I have feels perfectly at home anywhere, anyhow or any fashion. Every one dreads the summer campaign. Our Surgeons know and appreciate Mrs. Lee's and my services very highly and if they alone had the power everything would be done to induce us to go. Mrs. Lee is anxious to go. I am sure I am not. I want to come home. I dread a battle awfully; somebody that I am attached to must suffer and I can tell you it is easier to see *strange* soldiers suffer than those you have lived with for nearly three months. Dr. Potter has been a prisoner in Richmond. Dr. Wolf has been there three times. I think it will be about Dudley's luck to go this summer. He is perfectly reckless in time of battle. Dr. Potter said Dudley was caring for the wounded right on the front when he was shot at Gettysburg. The Sanitary Com. made me a present of a side saddle, one a secesh had to leave behind; it is not a very splendid one. A tailor in one of the wards has been putting two skirts together and tomorrow I am to have a ride on Lieut. Fogg's horse. When the 12th N. J. have their new colors presented I am going over to see them. Dr. Miller is going to take me. We had two English celebrities, a Surgeon and Colonel, in the English Navy, here a few days since. I am real sleepy so will conclude with love to thee and father. I remain thy affectionate daughter

CORNELIA HANCOCK
late *3rd Div. 2 A.C.*

Capt. Mattison just returned from leave of absence, said Ann Pancoast sent her love to me, suddenly risen in importance have I not!

Direct care of Dr. W. W. Potter, Surg. in charge 1st Div. 2 Corps hospt.

Near Brandy Sta., Va.

V

THE BATTLE OF THE WILDERNESS

✿

. . . When General Grant took command of the Army of the Potomac all civilians were ordered to leave the Army. I returned to Philadelphia, but remained only a short time, for going on an errand to 7th & Arch one day I heard the newspaper boys crying "The Battle of the Wilderness," and "General Hays killed." I did not finish my errand, but went home and told Ellen I was going to Washington that night and *did go,* to find Washington in the same suspense and uncertainty that prevailed in Philadelphia after the battle of Gettysburg. Hospital supplies and nurses had been sent to meet the Army in its distress, but had to return, not being able to make connection with the Army by land. Then preparations were made to go by the Potomac River. Confusion and uncertainty marked everything, and when I went to the Secretary of War for a pass he thought things were in too much chaos to grant it. I thought differently and started off with Doctor,[1] as his assistant, every physician being allowed one, and my being a *woman* was *not* noted on the pass; so I was soon again inside the lines. The steamboats on the Potomac were loaded with supplies and dispatched to Belle Plain to return with wounded.

[To Ellen from her Husband Dr. Henry T. Child]

On board the Wawasset, *Aquia Creek, at Belle Plain*
4th day after noon, May 12th, 1864.
WE arrived here yesterday at 5 P. M. and I was set to work at once placing the wounded men on the boat. More than 3,000 were sent to

[1] Her brother-in-law, Dr. Child.

83

Washington this afternoon. This morning Surgeon Cuyter detailed me to go in the boat, which is Eddie Taggert's, with 527 wounded men—many very bad cases. We were about 2 hours getting them on board and I have been engaged ever since dressing the wounds. They are almost all in good spirits and are far better than in cars. I drew an order for 250 rations—that was 500 loaves of bread, 250 lbs of cooked meat, and in 2 hours it had all disappeared. I only stay a little while in Washington while we unload the men & take in the coal. Many of the men are badly burned; the woods were on fire and hundreds of the wounded burned, especially the Rebels, who had no friends to assist them, were burned to death. It has been and is the most fearful battle of modern times and perhaps of any time. It is computed we shall have 30,000 wounded men, those who have come in have been mostly slightly wounded. I met Eddie Taggert on the wharf & he invited Cornelia & me to stay on the Boat. We put up tents & got a fire going & Cornelia was the first and *only* woman there yesterday. Today the Sanitary Com have 2 women here. Before we had been here an hour Cor. had a barrel of coffee made and the poor fellows were mostly fed. I left C. on the wharf and went to assist the wounded on the boat out to a large boat. We got through at 10 o'clock I went on shore to hunt Cornelia but she had gone to Fredericksburg—so I went back and went to bed in the cabin. At 12 o'c. 900 more had arrived and were put on the boat to go out to the Wenona which could not get up to the wharf. We did not get them all on board till 5 o.c. this morning. I slept several hours in the cabin. I was wakened about 4 o.c. by a cry of "a man over board"— by means of the lanterns we could see, and a rope being cast out he was rescued.

There is a vast amount of necessary work here and now the officials have broken most of the red tape, any good worker is welcome. I have been most cordially received by every officer and man and I don't know that I shall go any farther.

You will hear of another terrible battle yesterday. We have a reporter for the Tribune on board—he came from Grant's H.Qtrs. this

84

WHARF AT BELLE PLAIN

morning at 6 o.c. He says there was a desperate battle and that our men pushed the enemy all day and now had the advantage of them.

I will write thee again soon.

from thy husband

H. T. CHILD

DEAR ELLEN [1]

IT is some date and I am in Fredericksburg city. I do not know where Doctor is. On going ashore at Belle Plain we were met with hordes of wounded soldiers who had been able to walk from the Wilderness battlefield to this point. They were famished for food and as I opened the remains of my lunch basket the soldiers behaved more like ravenous wolves than human beings, so I felt the very first thing to be done was to prepare food in unlimited quantities, so with my past experience in arranging a fire where there seemed no possibility of one, I soon had a long pole hanging full of kettles of steaming hot coffee, and this, with soft bread, was dispensed all night to the tramping soldiers who were filling the steam boats on their return trip to Washington. Soon the long train of ambulances containing severely wounded men commenced arriving and among them the Head Qts. ambulance with Gen. Hays' dead body on its way to Pittsburg. I knew this ambulance had to report back to the 2nd Corps Hospital and when daylight came Dr. Detmold and Dr. Vanderpool, two eminent surgeons of New York, and I boarded it to go to Fredericksburg, where our hospital is established. On arriving here the scenes beggared all description and these two men, eminent as they are in their profession, were paralyzed by what they saw. Rain had poured in through the bullet-riddled roofs of the churches until our wounded lay in pools of water made bloody by their seriously wounded condition. On these scenes Dr. Detmold and Dr. Vanderpool gazed in horror and seemed not to know where to take hold. My Gettysburg experience enabled me to take hold. The next morning these two

[1] Her sister.

85

surgeons came to me and said: "If we open another church under better conditions than these, will you accompany us?" and I said "Yes." After they got their nerve their splendid executive ability asserted itself and they had the pews knocked to pieces; under the backs and seats put a cleat and made little beds to raise the wounded from the floor. 'Tis true the beds have no springs, but it keeps them from lying in the water. Here day by day things are improving. An amputating table is improvised under a tree in the yard where these two good men work indefatiguably.

Fredericksburg, Va.

MY DEAR MOTHER

I WAS the first and only Union woman in the city. I believe today there were some of Miss Dix's nurses came thru. I have good quarters. We calculate there are 14,000 wounded in the town; the Secesh help none, so you may know there is suffering equal to any thing anyone ever saw, almost as bad as Gettysburg, only we have houses and churches for the men. I am well, have worked harder than I ever did in my life; there was no food but hard tack to give the men so I turned in and dressed their wounds. It was all that could be done. I hear from my friends at the front one by one. Almost every one I knew was shot dead except the Doctor. Some of them are taken prisoners, Dr. Aiken for one; Dr. Dudley was safe last night. Lieut. Fogg was shot dead, so was Capt. Madison—this battle is still raging. I am glad I am here but I really thought my heart would break as one after another they told me was dead. If they only accomplish getting to Richmond. If not, it is a dear battle. There is very heavy firing today. I hope Dr. Dudley will get thru safe. He sent a Doctor to see me, told him he knew I would get thru. He is out on the front with his Regt. Oh, how awful, it seems as if the great judgment day was upon us now; the Secesh are still in town but we take possession of all churches and houses we want. I am well. Write to me in care of Dr. Davis, 1st Div. 2nd Corps hospt., Fred'ksburg, Va.

I ought not to be writing here now, but Guerrillas were very thick

86

the first night the trains were captured and we could not get up to Fredksburg, but the next morning went thru with a cavalry escort. The news is very rejoicing this morning but we never believe anything here. Suffering, suffering, but the men are in good spirits as we appear to be gaining. I chartered a new hospital today. The Surg. Gen. of N. York has charge of it and it is now in shape. The other hospt. in town are shocking in filth and neglect. Ours is the best. I wish all in Fredericksburg and beyond were as comfortable as ours are. Tonight the news that reaches us is good and the men even when badly wounded shout and cheer. I am going out on the front to our new div. hospit. in a few days but you need not be concerned. If we are victorious I shall be all right. Any way I shall be all right. Our hospt. here will be all right in a few days and we can do more good on the battlefield. I am permanently calculated for getting along under very trying circumstances. The firing has been most terrific today. The loss in officers is very great. Gen. Welt was brought in today. The first night I got here I slept in Gen. Hays' ambulance, the one that brought his body to Aquia Creek. Mrs. Lee is sick I believe. I believe she would arise from a sick bed and come down if she knew what a condition their hospt. was in. You must write. I am very well and all right. I have never seen Dr. since he landed at Aquia Creek.

Thine in haste

CORNELIA HANCOCK

Fredericksburg, Va., May 14, 1864.

MY DEAR SISTER

I KNOW not what I have written and I scarcely know that I shall write intelligibly now, but I write that I am this moment writing in a splendid house of an F.F.V. I came here to see some of the officers of the 12 N. J. with Dr. Miller who came from the front and made a B line for me on reaching here. He reports Dr. Dudley doing well at the front for which I am very thankful. This battle is perfectly frightful in its havoc. I burst out crying the moment I saw Dr. Miller. It filled

87

my mind with Lieut. Fogg's death. Capt. Madison's body was not found. We have our men tolerably comfortable now but it is the only hospital. Consequently the gentleman who has charge of this has been chosen to take care of a general hospital to be established at the Lacy house. He is ex-surgeon genl. of N. York. He is honest enough to admit that I have done much toward its success, and confers the honor of making me boss of his new hospt. I do not know that I shall accept. I want to stay with our Div. Poor contrabands hardly catch a thought in these wonderful times. We have scarcely anything to eat. I have had nothing but hard tack and tea since I came. The wounded also are suffering for food as the trains are all taken up carrying forage and ammunition to the front. I never was better in my life: certain I am in my right place. I live with a Secesh woman who is very polite to me, as their living depends upon being so while we hold possession. It seems like the day of Judgment. We have several generals in town. The soldiers are in the highest of spirits. I went into a dark, loathsome store house, the floor smeared with molasses, found about twenty wounded who had not had their wounds dressed for twenty-four hours and had ridden some fifteen or twenty miles. O, God! such suffering it never entered the mind of man or woman to think of. There are many more than at Gettysburg, in one respect it is better than there: we have dry houses.

From thy sister—C. HANCOCK

Fredericksburg, Va., May 20, 1864.

MY DEAR SISTER

WE have an awful time here. Have to submit to seeing the men fed with hard tack and coffee. Supplies are very limited, scarcely any soft bread reached us. There is no end to the wounded, they arrive any time, night or day. Guerrilas infest the country and endeavor to cut off our supplies going to the front. I have written very little. It is impossible to get time to write. I board with a Secesh family. They are very civil to us because they know they have to be, but I can tell you they are bitter Secesh. I hope the North does not feel jubilant over our successes for we have little cause so far. It seems to be Grant's determination to persist if he is whipped, and I can assure any one he *is* whipped about half his time, but does not appear to care. The suffering does not seem so great as at Gettysburg because they are in houses. But I have not seen near the worst as my hospt. was started first under the auspices of the Surg. Gen. of N. Y. and has taken the lead of any in the town. Dr. is in Fredericksburg now, he has done much service to Belle Plains. I received thy letter tonight. Direct a letter to me 1st Div. 2nd Corps hospital, Fredericksburg, Va. and it will come as the doctors change so often there is no telling who will be in charge. Dr. Aiken has been a prisoner for about two weeks. He was released and I saw him today and I tell you I was glad. He is nearly starved. Dr. Dudley was within an ace of being with him. He is still alive and with his Regt. He sent me a note today that he would come in to see me as soon as possible. Col. More, his friend, lies wounded here. I have seen Dr. Miller; Dr. Potter is at the front and Dr. Rowland too. Abbe Gibbons is here, & Mrs. Harris, but I must pride myself I was the first on the spot. Mrs. Swisshelm and Miss Willetts are here, came on my pass, and are doing excellent service. I want this letter sent to mother. As to writing any thing to show the public, I cannot do it. The publick must know that Fredericksburg is one vast hospital requiring all the muscle and supplies the North can send. The groans go up from every building. The Rebel wounded we have not here. Lieut. Fogg and Capt. Madison I still grieve much for. I wish I had them here *wounded*. I take care of Col. More, 14 Conn. and three officers of the 12 N. J.

I hope you will write. I know many interesting things I might tell you of the Secesh, but it is nearly midnight and I must conclude.

C. HANCOCK

A man's artery has just started. I ran for a doctor, and looking at my watch it is 12 o'clock.

89

May 21st, 1864.

MY DEAR MOTHER

I HAVE written very little to any one since I have been here. There has been no suitable time. The suffering here beggars all description, only better than Gettysburg because we do not have to leave them on the ground. It is worse because they fight every day. The wounds are terrible. I do not see Grant has accomplished much, yet he fights right straight ahead whether he gets any advantage or not. Guerrillas infest the country all around, not one mile from here. Capt. Williams and Brooks, Lieut. Brown & Phipps were all wounded. I have been seeing after them considerable. We have about one hundred and fifty in this hospital. I am considered one of the most efficient women in Fredericksburg which is a satisfaction when one has to work as hard as I do. The Surg. Genl. of N. York started this hospital but he has left now. Dr. Dwinelle is at the front. I have not seen him. Dr. Dudley wrote me a note stating he would come to see me as soon as possible, but could not leave while his Regt. was fighting. Many officers of his Regt. are wounded, lying round, and he himself lost his sword, belt and instruments, but says he is thankful for his life. I am writing this in the hospt. it is in a Methodist church, not a spot on the floor but a wounded hero is lying. They complain very little although they lie on the hard boards.

90

VI

ON MARCH WITH THE ARMY
TO WHITE HOUSE LANDING

✿

May 28th, 1864.

MY DEAR SISTER

IT is one of the most beautiful mornings that ever blew. We are just evacuating Fredericksburg, the wounded having been all sent to Washington. We had the pleasure of feeding the wounded who were kept prisoners in the Wilderness for nearly three weeks and almost starved. I met a surg. who asked me why the cavalry had not released them before and wanted to know what was going to be done with them. I told him they most of them had been sent back to the regt. in the front. He filled with tears and said they could not send *him* as he had but eleven men left in his Regt. I never felt more sorry for a man. The men, prepared for march, about 8,000, are all in line with shining bayonets. The cavalry, all mounted officers, riding up and down the line, flags waving, everything around is exhilarating. They go about one hundred yards, then halt. A courier who just brought in a dispatch from Gen. Grant is guarding our wagon. He is an intelligent German and goes out to the farm houses and gets us fresh milk and cakes. He is the most splendid rider I ever saw and is as brave as he can be. He had his horse shot under him yesterday but soon captured another, says he will try to get one for me before we arrive at Port Royale. We have a battery at the front of the train and Cavalry on all sides, still they say the guerrillas have attacked the rear of the train and captured fourteen men and killed two. Poor soldiers. It is very hard on a march. They are constantly falling by

91

the roadside. I have carried lots of their guns and knapsacks for them today. I felt many times like giving them my seat. I can enjoy myself in a march looking round. There is always something going on interesting and most of the time I can sleep in the most profound manner. They shoot the chickens, calves, pigs, and &c then lay them along the road and every man gets a stick and shoulders a piece. We stopped for dinner and have seen nothing of Grant's messenger since. I guess he has been gobbled by Guerrillas. Every few rods a man sings out: "There is Miss Hancock." Mrs. Lee is a very good singer. It is getting towards night and she is singing as we are wearily nearing Port Royale. In this town we cannot obtain any resting place except in the negro shanties but that does not concern my mind at all. We have a hoe cake for supper and no prospect for breakfast.

May 30th—we staied in P. Royal all night in some negro quarters and this morning went to the Medical Director's office and heard from time to time that no passes were to be granted to any *ladies* except for them to *return* to *Washington*. I sat upon my trunk perfectly easy. There has always been a way provided and I always expect there will be, so never concern. At length a doctor comes up who volunteers us to go on the transport *without* a pass. That I often do. But I like going in the wagon train better and the Sanitary have offered to carry us thru, so now I am sitting in their wagon. We have plenty of provisions with us and I hope will get thru comfortably. They are making wounded all the time and our services will be needed by the time we get there. I hope you are doing well at home but I have had no tidings that you are as I have never received a letter except one from Ellen. Capt. Harris has just come, volunteers us to be as comfortable as possible.

Direct a letter to Miss Hancock
care of Sanitary Comm.
White House, V.

This morning this place is to be evacuated and the White House is to be the next base. Oh! what a sight. This place was one mass of tired, swearing soldiery, scrambling for a hard tack, killing chickens,

92

ARMY WAGON TRAIN

IN VIRGINIA

pigs, calves &c. Seems like Bedlam let loose. I am always cared for tho'; before we had been in the town half an hour a guard was detailed over the house, so we slept in perfect security. I hope Grant is accomplishing something as he is making terrible suffering for the rear of his army. They never have been used to rapid evacuating and advancing into an enemy's country. The White House sounds nearer to Richmond. I shall always remember with pleasure some Secesh I met in Fredericksburg. I believe we are to have a Johnny cake for breakfast. I have always been well received where I am known and if I could be allowed to stay with them would be content to make few new acquaintances. I do not wish you to give a thought of uneasiness for me. I am always contented with my lot and if *you* will not concern I will promise you *I* will not. I would give lots to see our children especially Eddie. Yesterday during the shelling a child not 3 years old walked across the commons. If thee knows anything of Salem affairs write me. I expect Dr. Potter has lots of letters for me from mother; direct in his care 1st Div. 2nd Corps Hospital. I want a letter awfully, and if you have done your duty there will be some at the front. I have no fear but you have for when I am here I long since have been convinced I have the best sister and mother in the world. If Dr. Aiken returns send my things.

With much love,

I am thy sister—CORNELIA

May 31st, 1864—On March.

MY DEAR SISTER

WE left Port Royale on the Rappahannock 15 miles below Fredericksburg on the 30th of May, Mrs. Lee, Georgy Willets and I having come here from that place in an open wagon the day before. Now we are on our march for the White House—a distance of about 45 miles though the roads are very winding and it may be much farther. It is a very warm day and the guards suffer very much with the dust and heat. There is almost always an alarm along the line about Guer-

93

rillas, often just enough to make a pleasant excitement. I cannot feel afraid and strange as it may seem the soldiers want to have a brush with them. I almost worship our faithful soldiers who trudge on and never murmur or complain. I am in a Sanitary spring wagon and it is very comfortable—when I get tired I can lie down and sleep. Mrs. Lee is a very pleasant travelling companion. The army has not passed through this section and there appears to have been some attempt at cultivating the land, but we would not consider that there was anything worth harvesting. We are eating strawberries, peas, &c—Tonight we halted at a village called Newtown, went into a Secesh house, found a nice bed and room to sleep. They told us they have nothing to eat. We sent back to the train for rations and had the colored people to get us a good supper which we ate upon their table. The women are bitter Secessionists—one said her husband is a commisary in the Rebel army. We think he furnishes rations to the guerilla bands and I was not disposed to show them any favours but true to some people's idea of right they wanted to take Sanitary stuff and give those rebels to live on because they said they were starving. There was a splendid side saddle that I wanted to confiscate for I know that has been smuggled from the North. There was not a man in our crowd who had spunk enough to take it. I wish Dr. Dudley had been along, I would have had it then. Protecting Secesh property is entirely played out with me.

June 1st.

At 7 o'clock this morning we left our Secesh enemies and resumed the march which was extremely dusty. After we had gone about a mile on the road the guerrilas made a dash, but our cavalry immediately drove them back into the woods. I never saw anything more promptly accomplished, not a gun was fired, yet the woods have been searched and not a rebel can be found. Our train this morning is 15 miles long and more expected to catch up. Even the colored people are Secesh here and we cannot induce them to go along with us. A few stragglers have joined the teams this morning. In Fredericksburg I never found a disaffected colored person. No one need

94

ever speak against Jersey, it is a paradise compared to Virginia. We rode on about a mile and found a house deserted, the owner of which was said to be a chief of Guerrillas, so the soldiers fired his house and it is now burning. Just beyond us, a line of our cavalry are chasing what appears to us a dosen mounted guerrillas. They have come in, however, finding only some colored people who say that there is a mounted guerrilla band 200 strong. Whether we will overtake them or not is a question. We have halted to water the train which is quite a job. If I ever get through this march safely I shall feel thankful. If not, I shall never regret having made the attempt for I am no better to suffer than the thousands who die. I think that the privates in the army who have nothing before them but hard marching, poor fare and terrible fighting are entitled to all the unemployed muscle of the North and they will get mine with a good will during this summer. Then if Grant does not take Richmond, I am afraid that I shall be discouraged. I can bear all I have witnessed in this campaign if we are only successful. We have, every day, evidences of the most distinguished gallantry of our troops and I know all they want is a leader and I hope that they will find him in Grant. The bridge over the Matapony is broken and we have to remain here about three hours. We hear the cannons dealing them deadly blows near Hanover Court House. I feel quite anxious to get out to the field but have started upon this Campaign possessing my mind with patience, and so I expect to try to continue. We have moved two or three hundred yards nearer the Matapony, over which the bridge is broken. If we cannot go on it is pleasant to rest. We make up our minds to anything that comes and so are not much disappointed. A few hours later finds us one and a half miles beyond the Matapony River around a poor white woman's house. She and her six children live in the most desolate wilderness. They have been plundered of all their eatables and she seemed forlorn indeed. Her husband died about a year ago. She is the nearest approach to a Union woman I have seen in Virginia. She is like the poor of our own neighborhood, only she wishes it settled in order that she may see better times. We left her plenty of supplies.

She treated us the best she could and now we have bid her adieu and are just starting out on another day's tramp, expecting to reach Hanover town. There is continued firing both front and rear, but we have been preserved so far. I hope to reach our Division hospital to-day and see who is wounded. There are two young men belonging to the Sanitary Commission, Mr. Clarence Messer and Charles Wycoff, who try to make the trip agreeable. The latter is a brother-in-law to the gentleman who vacated the Chancellor's house and made his escape with his family to the North.

White House, June 3rd—I arrived at this place yesterday having joined a train of wounded coming from the battle field with Dr. Aiken. We got opposite the White House and found no bridge and were obliged to keep our wounded in ambulance 12 hours longer, making two days and nights they have been loaded and on the way. I have turned wound-dresser and cleaner generally. You can hardly imagine the appearance of our wounded men now brought in from the field, after having been under fire for 20 successive days. They hardly look like men but are extremely hopeful that Richmond will be taken. There are lots of women; but I seem to be still in favour in the 2nd Corps and certainly please the wounded men. Dr. Burmeister is in charge here. Dr. Aiken transports the wounded from the field. Dr. Dudley sends me letters but I do not see him. He is at a Division Hospital in the field. Such fighting never was recorded in any history. I hope the people are behaving in a becoming manner at the North for we are wearing sackcloth here, there is so much suffering. We hear the firing night and day, one continued belching forth of artillery. Miss Willets is here, very sick at present. I think it a cause of great thankfulness that I am preserved in health and strength. Mrs. Lee has a cooking shanty up and is therefore happy. I am not cooking, but have a ward and do everything else, which suits me better. I have no more knowledge whether you fare well or ill at home than if I was in my grave, but I hope that I shall receive letters now if they are directed White House, Virginia, care of the Sanitary Commission.

If any body feels an interest to send anything to me in care of the Sanitary Commission, it would be forwarded. I am certain that if the ladies of the North knew how important pads are to us they would send more than we now get. It is impossible to get beds and blankets sufficient and pads afford us great relief. Remember me to everybody. I am afraid I shall be old and gray by the time you see me again, but if I surrender my life it will not be as valuable as thousands of brave men who are falling hereabouts. Send all I write to Mother immediately with the request that she copy it in ink. I want my letters preserved as I keep no other diary. Give my love to the children. I have met with one loss; my photograph album was stolen or lost in the march and I regret the loss.

From thy sister

C. HANCOCK

[From her Sister Ellen]

634 Race St. Philada., June 5th, 1864.

MY DEAR CORNELIA

I HOPE thee does not think we have been neglectful of thee. We have been looking for word from thee—so that we might send thee a letter with some certainty of thy getting it. Mrs. Richards got home and reported that Mrs. Lee and thee had gone on with the army—I have tried to frighten my self about thee but do not make out much. Dr. got home and has been well ever since. I do not know that thee has heard that William has got a commission and going out for 100 days. He is here now and the company are at Trenton where he is going tomorrow. There has been a very good articale published in the N. Y. Tribune[1] and an Albany paper about thee—signed "V." Dr. says

---

[1] New York *Tribune* of May 31st, 1864: "All day (the first of her arrival) Miss Hancock worked assiduously in her sphere. When the next day I opened a new hospital at the Methodist Church, I invited her to accompany me. She did so, and if success attended the efforts to ameliorate the sufferings it was in no small degree owing to her indefatigable labors. Within an hour one hundred and twenty men had been placed in the building and she had seen that good beef soup had been administered to each, and during the period I was there no deli-

97

that he supposes that Dr. Vanderpool wrote it. He gives thee great credit and I shall send it to thee as soon as I think there is any probability of thy getting it. We are very hopeful alltho we do not forget the fearful price the poor soldier is paying. I hope to hear from thee every mail and shall be very uneasy if we do not before long. Mrs. Dudley sent a letter of thanks for the picture. I will send it to thee soon. I think I shall answer it and send her word, how her son was on the 18th of May as she said that she hoped thee would write if thee knew, for she had not heard for some time.

Mr. Owen is sitting with me. He keeps saying thee is a real *heroine*. Every body says that the articale in the paper was good, and seem delighted to know me on account of my *sister*. Josiah Wilson says that thee was very highly spoken of on the Freedman Committee the other day and that they are going to send to Washington soon about it.

With much love, I remain

thy sister   E. M. CHILD

Hospital 1st Div. 2nd Corps, Va.
June 7th, 1864

MY DEAR MOTHER

FOR the first time since I started from home I am at leisure and enjoying myself highly. I left White House Sta. at the urgent solicitation of Mrs. Maj. Genl. Barlow to visit the front with the view of

cacy or nutriment attainable was wanting to the men. Were any dying, she sat by to soothe their last moments, to receive the dying messages to friends at home, and when it was over, to convey by letter the sad intelligence. Let me rise ever so early, she had already preceded me at work; and during the many long hours of the day she never seemed to weary or flag. In the evening, when all in her own hospital had been fully cared for, she would go about the town with delicacies to administer to those who were so situated that they otherwise could not obtain them. At night she sought a garret (and it was literally one) for rest. One can but feebly portray the ministration of such a person. She belonged to no association, and had no compensation. She commanded respect, for she was lady-like and well educated; so quiet and undemonstrative that her presence was scarcely noticed except by the smiling faces of the wounded as she passed."

98

establishing a feeding station for the wounded on their road in from the front hospital to the rear hospital. I came with her in her husband's head qt. ambulance and have now penetrated as *near Richmond* as any lady in the Army. Much to our disappointment we find the wounded are all *shipped* to the rear hospt. Consequently, there is nothing to do. The head-qts. hospt. is in a Virginia mansion and I am back *home* with Dr. Potter and Aiken & Dr. Dudley. One after another they come in to see me, and I am luxuriating on a back piazza overlooking a splendid garden of flowers, the birds singing beautifully and the air splendid. There is no firing this morning which is a relief as it has been one incessant roar. The only thing that is painful to witness is the thinness of my friends. Dr. Dudley is a shadow comparatively speaking, and so with all the rest. They say they are well but worked down. Dr. Potter has given me my choice of rooms and I have chosen one opening right off the piazza. If we can only stay here I shall be so glad and have a pleasant place to receive the wounded in. The hospital at the White House had 1650 wounded in when I left. The Surg. said Mrs. Barlow might pick out any ten women or any two surgeons and take along with her if she would leave *me*. There is an embalmed Lieutenant on the piazza awaiting transportation or there would be nothing around to remind us of war. Mrs. Barlow has gone to Div. Head Qts to see her husband and I am the only Lady round. There are several contrabands, however. I receive no letters whatever nor ever have since I left home except one from Ellen. I do not even know whether you receive mine. I hope you do. I take it for granted you are doing well and you may have some anxiety in regard to me. I have great faith, however, that I shall go through safely though sometimes exposed to danger. Drs. Dudley, Miller and Rowland have been talking with me for an hour & it seems really like old times. A flag of truce is out after our wounded who are between the lines and I am in hopes they will find them. I hope you do not feel elated and think Grant is doing great things for it is not the case; the wise feel great doubts about taking Richmond and it is true he is not as far as McClellan was. Yet I hope

99

for the best but know that we have sustained severe loss and gained very little as yet. Mrs. Barlow is going to bed. The band has been sent for and is playing Yankee Doodle.

I have a nice ingrain carpet, a trundle bed, a large arm chair, a wash stand, towel rack, basin & pitcher, a bureau of cottage furniture, a nice rocking chair, &c. Very luxurious, I assure you. If we can only stay here, but the orders may come tonight to move. A shell explodes every little while not far away; about as much account is made of it as the dropping of a pin at home. Habit is a wonderfull matter.

June 8th, 1864—We have sent every wounded man away from the hospital. I have nothing to do but enjoy myself. Hostilities have ceased for the present and Mrs. Barlow and I are rusticating. It is perfect weather. I hope I shall have a letter from you. Direct care of Dr. W. W. Potter, 1st Div. 2nd Corps Hosptl. It is now the night of the 8th of June. Mrs. Barlow has gone to the Genl. Head Qtrs. and will be back tomorrow with orders from him whether to go to the rear or front. I can do whatever she does. Dr. Potter is the same gentleman that he ever was, and wants I should go right along with the ambulance train. Have you seen the "Tribune" of the 31st—quite a dissertation upon "Miss Cornelia Hancock." It was sent to me the same day from two sources. I think very good fortune always awaits me for some reason or other. I hope it will continue. I want this letter copied in ink and preserved, and this one sent to Ellen.

from thy affectionate daughter,

CORNELIA

Give much love to father, Sallie, Will, B. Tell the children they must write to me and some time I will answer it.

1st Div. 2nd Corps Hospt.
June 9, 1864.

MY DEAR SISTER

I WROTE to mother yesterday and requested her to send thee the letter

100

but as I have continued leisure I might as well write to thee to say at last I am at home with all my old Doctors around. Dr. Potter is as polite as ever and Dr. Rowland smokes his pipe. Dr. Dudley seemed glad to see me, the only trouble I have with him is he will go up on the breast works at the front for no other reason than to see, and some of these times he will be brought in dead or wounded. Last night he got fast in a place where he had to lie for three quarters of an hour before he could venture out. All my friends are very thin. It is painful to see them though they say they are perfectly well. We are enjoying a lull in hostilities. I suppose the North is clamoring "on to Richmond" still, but I fear it will be some time yet before the clamor will cease. The most trouble I see— I had written thus far and was called off and have forgotten what "the trouble" was, so I guess it was not much account. I just received thy letter dated June 5. I hope you have received intelligence of my whereabouts before this. There is no call for being frightened about me, they seldom shell a *hospital* and if they did it does not follow they would pick me out to shoot.

I am glad Dr. is well. Is it not wonderful I am well. I have gone thru much more than I ever did before. I am sorry Thomas is sick and feel glad I had him eat his dinner with Dr. Aiken before he left us. I am not surprised that William has gone forth again. I should do the same if I were a man. Playing soldier is all past with Grant. I hope they do not enlist thinking they will not have to leave Washington, for if Grant wants them in the front Rifle pits he will have them. He has ordered all the poor little drummer boys to shoulder muskets and go into the Rifle pits. He has no more right to order them in than to order any other *attache* of the Army. I told Genl. Barlow today it was unjust.

Write me all about William. What Regt., what rank, where ordered, &c. How to direct a letter and &c. Mr. Barlow and another gentleman sent me the paper containing the report of my hospt. in Fredericksburg. Dr. Vanderpool wrote it. I want you to know the rebels and our men are not farther apart than across your parlor, *face to face*. No men can raise their heads without being shot. Dr. Dudley said he saw a man raise his head once or twice and thought to tell him to lay low, but did not and in a few hours he was brought into the hospital—shot thru the head. A man cannot even go to the spring to get some water without being shot. We average about six per day shot on such expeditions. Send me Mrs. Dudley's letter. I will answer it. It would be well if thee had written but now he has written himself and I will answer the one she wrote me. Dr. Dudley got a letter from her stating they had great anxiety for him and saying they had been up the St. Mary's River and fired, themselves, two canons at the Rebs. Mother must feel pretty badly with both her children gone to war. There are many people of the same opinion with Mr. Owen. Give my love to him. Poor Freedmen—we have lots of them here today.

June 10th—I am well and perfectly happy. I want you to write direct 1st Div. 2nd Corps Hospt. care of Dr. W. W. Potter, be careful to put W. W. for there is a George L. I have received still an other paper with the Tribune notice, so thee need not send it to me. Capt. Derickson of Gen. Barlow's staff, gave it to me this morning. Mrs. Barlow and I expect to remain with the hospt. department and follow along with the rest. Rodman & Lym Smith were here this morning both well. Every body comes here almost. Dr. Dudley is going to move his tent up out of the woods this morning. If we stay we shall soon be splendidly fixed. Thee may think I am now, if I say I have a nice bed, clean white sheets, a rosewood bureau, wash stand, towel rack, rocking and arm chairs; the gentlemen sleep in their tents and all the furniture is concentrated in my room. I have two little nigs to wait on me and have an easy time generally, comparing it with White House, or Fredericksburg.

The Rebs. gave our men tobacco when the flag of truce was up, but they will shoot with a vigor when ordered.

Thine in haste

CORNELIA HANCOCK

White House, June 12.

MY DEAR SISTER

DR. AIKEN is ordered to Phila to be mustered out and will visit you. I shall send some things home by him which I want carefully put away. I am afraid I will loose them carrying them around. Dr. Dudley has charge of the ambulance train now. He will want me to spend my energies in his hospital now, but I shall stand by the first Div. I want no better treatment than I receive at Dr. Potter's hands. Anything you want to know of me Dr. Aiken can tell you. If he returns I would like to have an apron and some new ruffles. I want a coarse comb very much. I have borrowed all Dr. Dudley's postage stamps so you had better send me some more; direct my letters 1st Div. 2nd Corps Hospt. care of W. W. Potter and do write soon. Tell me about William. I am well and happy. The only bad thing about me I have no faith in taking Richmond. Gen. Barlow is to be appointed Chief of Freedman's Bureau. He is just the man and I know him quite well and would not hesitate to get Will a position if war only passes. Edward Parish met me today on the Sanitary boat. I would like some sewing tackle. I am at the White House landing awaiting transportation to Harrison's Landing. I have been very near cannonading but they have not disturbed me at all. Mrs. Lee is working hard. White House is evacuated now.

from thy sister

CORNELIA

[From her Mother]

6th mo. 13th 1864.

DEAR CORNELIA

I AM inclined to write frequently to thee fearing thee will not get near all my letters. The piece published in the Salem paper extracted from the New York "Daily Tribune" is creating a sensation in this neighborhood. It has reminded me of a scripture passage "When a man's ways please the Lord he maketh even his enemies to be at peace

103

with him," as those who we used to consider thy enemies are foremost in extolling thee now. Aunt Ruth says Nelly always *was* a good nurse. William Bradway says not *one* in a *thousand* could perform so much. Mary has so many beautiful things to say I cannot remember them, but closed with saying she hoped thee would not break down under the work in which desire I most sincerely join.

I intend to mail a Salem Standard to thee. It brings in all the family but Ellen. I think she should have been noticed as the wife of Dr. Child! William has been at home several days but went to Trenton today. He has all his men but 11 and is to be Captain.

Everything around here looks very beautiful and if this cruel war could be brought to an honorable close I should feel very thankful and happy. The Sanitary Fair is flourishing.

I conclude thy

Affectionate

MOTHER

White House, June 15, 1864.

MY DEAR MOTHER

I RECEIVED a letter from thee a few days ago, which is the first word I have had from thee since I left Philadelphia. I hope thee received a letter containing a description of a 4 days march which I made from Fredericksburg to White House. I have been there ever since except one week which Mrs. Gen. Barlow and myself spent up at the front. When last I wrote I expected to go on the March with Dr. Potter's hospital but the orders were countermanded on account of two other ladies applying for the same privilege. We returned to the White House and found them evacuating slowly. The ladies have all embarked for Harrisons Landing on board the transports. Mrs. Lee got very tired of our last overland march, so she went on the boats and Mrs. Husbands and I are going in the train with Capt. Harris of the San. Com. Sheridan's cavalry is expected in tonight and tomorrow we hope to start and get across to Harrisons Landing ahead of the boats. Capt. Harris has pitched us a nice little wall tent and in

WHITE HOUSE LANDING

it I have been sleeping the livelong day, writing and eating at intervals. Soldiering is a very uncertain life, some times so lazy one can hardly pass the time, then have to work night and day. I never feel like writing like I used to for some reason. The embalmer, a Mr. Wadsworth, has quite a handsome carriage and horses here and in that we have ridden as far as Guerillas would allow. The blacks have thrown up high breastwork here so if the army has to retreat, we will have them to fall back into. The Pamunkey River is filled with transports carrying troops somewhere but I know not where. There never was a place like the army where one absolutely knows nothing except what transpires in your immediate vicinity, for if you hear anything of what happens a few rods off if you sift the information you will find most of it rumor. I have met with one great loss, that is my photograph album. I think of it every day and wish I could find it. The 67th Reg. Penna. is now passing. Every man has a shining musket and many of them a frying pan stuck in their muskets. The Guerillas have just captured a few men and wounded some. The men have just run out announcing Sheridan's arrival with the Cavalry Corps. If so, we shall start tomorrow. I met with Anna Etheridge, who has been in the army for three years. She looks as sunburned as any soldiers. She has never left the field till part of the men went home on Veteran leave, when she accompanied them as far as Washington. She returned in the transports to her Regt., the third Michigan infantry. I never rec'd the letters sent to Fredericksburg. I heard from William through a gentleman from Trenton. I want you to be sure to send me the poetry on Lieut. Fogg. I shall never cease to regret his death. Dr. Dudley saw him just before he was shot; one of his boys he was going to operate upon had one of the Lieutenant's handkerchiefs on his wound. He tried to get it for me to keep but the boy set store by it and would not give it up. I never saw more magnificent flowers than I saw in the Secesh town of Fredericksburg. Tell Sally I shall be very glad to go to Richmond but have no faith in having that pleasure. I think Beulah had better go to the Fair. I hope she will be as courageous as she was before. I feel in hopes that

105

the 100 day men will not be called into active service. *June 16th*—we are still at White House awaiting the cavalry perfectly idle, we cannot walk a mile in circuit for Guerillas. There is no stir in camp, there was one man killed on picket today.

June 18th—Still at the White House. We went to the neighboring Regt. and found about 30 sick men and that will keep us busy for a while. I am well for which I should be very thankful.

Thy affectionate daughter

CORNELIA

White House, June 18, 1864.

MY DEAR SISTER

I DO think it very forlorn not to be able to receive any letters but such is the case in this disconsolate region of country. We are carefully cared for, however, by gentlemen of the Sanitary Com who volunteered to carry two of us over land to the new base. If there is no fighting I am very glad to be here.

Mrs. Husbands is doing for sick people in the 13 Ohio Cavalry Regt. I do not know that thee knows her, thee has heard me speak of her, she lives in that peculiar looking house corner of 18th and Spruce. She is even preferable to Mrs. Lee for a companion for me. She is a woman of the same indomitable perseverance and much more cultivated manners than Mrs. Lee. Tho I will never say aught against Mrs. Lee, as she has always been a friend to me. Cannonading can be distinctly heard. Have Henry, Morris, and Jones been ordered to join the Potomac Army? I heard yesterday they had; to hear from them in any way would be great satisfaction, you well may know. Direct all letters to me in care of W. W. Potter, Surg. in Charge of 1st Div. 2nd Corps Hospt. If you direct them to 1st Div. 2nd Corps they go up to the front any way and if they are in his care he is responsible for them. Things, too, remain in more order in the front than in the rear where there is such constant change of base. I got my letters while I was there and one thru the Sanitary Com. and the rest of the

106

information of your proceedings I have gathered from individuals roaming over the hospital. The news is at present that we start to night in the train. Sheridan's cavalry has appeared. You must feel no concern for me as I am in good hands. I will write as soon as I get somewhere.

Write to me and give my love to all.

thy sister
CORNELIA H.

VII

UNDER SHELL FIRE

✿

June 20th, 1864.

MY DEAR SISTER

THIS morning arose from my tent in a very pleasant frame of mind and ate my breakfast, when a soldier stepped up and said: "Hark! That is the long Roll," and in a few minutes the 67th Penn^a and a Colored Regiment were in the Rifle Pits in line of Battle. I walked out with Mrs. Husbands and talked with an intelligent colored Sergeant. He said they intended to show the Rebels no quarter. I encouraged them very strongly and retired to my tent. Capt. Harris came in and said he would not be the first to hitch up. A Mr. Wadsworth came and told us a man had just been shot through the lungs. We went out and dressed his wounds and were returning to put him in our tent when the Captain met us and said: "We have got to get out of this as quick as a flash." The Rebels opened a volley upon our pickets and cannon poured into them, tho' with little effect. Our tent was struck, baggage packed, and Mr. Wadsworth, who had a Germantown wagon, invited us to ride with him. All the teams were hitched up and we started with the rest of a long wagon train (the which the Rebels were after), went about a mile in circuit and parked, and in less than no time shot and shell fell very lively in our midst. Being civilians we attempted to go to the river bank when a shell struck right in the rear of our wagon, but on we went. There was no retreat then, and down to the water's edge behind a high bank. There Capt. Harris rode in, having been on that Common errand among my friends, a "looking round to see." He immediately rode to his wagon train and, I believe, was the means of saving his

108

team drivers from demoralization which they were fast getting into when we left them. In a short time he came back to us and advised us to get out of the wagon and walk along the river's edge and get over the bridge. A poor, demoralized gentleman (that is, he was sick) was sent with us, and along this bank for one half mile we went, the shot from our Gun boats and also from the Rebel batteries playing over us. On we trudged tho' through briars, mud, etc. I must speak disrespectfully of one party which encumbered my way; they were the cowardly officers who were crouching so closely to the bank and had their horses so in our way that sometimes I had to start them up and run under their heads to pass. The only inconvenience I felt from the trip was when our Gunboats fired, I was not 50 yards from them and the concussion made me yield obedience and make a very courteous bow at every report. At the bridge there was a captain and Lieut. (swearing, of course). I said we would sit down until the Sanitary appeared. He said we would get on the first thing we came to and ride across. I jumped onto a blacksmith's forge which looks like a gun carriage and made a safe skedaddle over the bridge. The Captn. told us to go to the Telegraph operator's office and await his arrival. Several arrangements were mentioned such as going on the Gunboats ahead with the wagons, &c. But if I ever am allowed to have my way I will obey what I am told in times of such confusion if I die in the attempt. Therefore, down we sat in the telegraph office the which I wish to explain the architecture of —a sandbank, a telegraph pole, and one instrument. But in the telegraph office we stayed. A Lieut., a friend of Mrs. Husbands', lent me a glass. The Telegraph operator set me at tearing up old dispatches and so time passed on and so did the ammunition & supply train of the Cavalry Corps. Soon Capt. Harris came up and reported he had lost four horses and had gained a wagon of forage; seemed well satisfied that all was well, as it was soon, too. Mr. Wadsworth with his carriage appeared and we got in and rode one half mile up, parked and had our dinner. The firing has ceased for the present and Sheridan with a whole Corps of Cavalry are

109

now passing us and we are again safe. A dustier looking party no one ever saw. We had some cherries and gave to them. They have travelled 25 miles. Every feeling with me accords honor and respect to their jaded countenances. I doubt if we do not look somewhat like them tomorrow night. What a monstrous body of men a Corps of Cavalry is. Its arriving will allow us to sleep much more securely in our beds than if they had not arrived. I suppose it will be chronicled as one of the mistakes that I stayed to go thru with the train. I am free to confess I was persistent, but of course could not foresee all this. I fear we have missed one week of service in the hospt. in Harrisons Landing, but of that we cannot know until we arrive there as we have been cut off from any information of any account since the 13 inst.

June 21st, 1864. Last evening we drew in to park in a field close to the Pamunkey River not 1/2 miles from yesterday's experience. A tent was erected for our accomodation and soon the same homelike appearance overspread the tenement that had characterized it in our previous encampment, as our table was spread upon the tail board of one of the wagons and our friends, Mr. Doolittle, Mr. Wadsworth, the Capt., Mrs. Husbands, & myself partook of a very good meal. Retired to rest upon a good bed and as thee well knows I have a good faculty to sleep, knew nothing until Six o'clock this morning. Arose, breakfasted with the same party, took a walk to the river bank, tried to descry Rebs with a glass but did not succeed, they having passed above some distance. Some stray firing, but hope they will so far annihilate them as to enable us to push forward. If I could hear from Will's proceedings it would give me great satisfaction, but I am determined to possess my mind with patience let what will come. The whole cavalry Corps came in here last night. Would it not have been splendid to have seen *Henry*. If he had only been in the Potomac Cavalry. Morris I have pretty much consigned to oblivion in my thoughts. Any one possessed of such fine talents as he and to use them to no better purpose in times of such opportunity for noble deeds, I think not worthy of my consideration. The 1st N. J. passed us, so if Jones had been in that I should have seen him. Everything happens just that contrary in the army. For uselessness, indolence, and all such adjectives give but an inadequate idea of the manner in which I have spent the last ten days. Yesterday was an adventure that, viewed in that light, may be a satisfaction, but it will be commented upon to my detriment as a faithful hospital *attendant*. The comments of the mass of people thee knows has very little effect upon my mind, however. The army is a great place to have violent friends or violent enemies, the one sometimes injuring you as much as the other. I ought not to complain, however.

Some real Jersey honeysuckles, brought to the carriage, fills the air with a more pleasant fragrance than is common upon a march. To park here has been ordered and splendid fresh spring water brought for us to wash in. Lieut. Beck has come up for his bitters. The Capt., too, to take *his ease*, I guess. A nap all round, and the artillery ordered to go out on the left. It is rather warm. God bless them, I say, when I see a soldier faithfully plodding through the dust protecting me. I feel more insignificant than words can express. Who would not help a soldier? Everything within me does honor to them. The parking is now over, and the use our wagon was during the parking was a sort of base for field officers whose whiskey had played out. A saddle has been confiscated by some of the train today at St. Charles City Court House. Nothing was to be seen but the densest clouds of smoke, a burning slave pen, and the ruins of the Court House. Stopped at a house just a little way beyond where the most wholesale destruction of property was going forward. I do not like to see wanton destruction but a dignified order to burn I enjoy and it is right, I believe. Went on about four miles and encamped, as it seems, in rather an uncertain place as our cavalry had been badly whipped the day before and we were too far from them to receive much protection. Encampment was of short duration however, as at nine in the evening the Capt. received orders to be in readiness to start in thirty minutes. Orders were obeyed and the train was ready to start in thirty minutes and remained in that state and did not move until four in the morning, sleeping as best we could—Mr. Wadsworth, Capt. Harris, Mrs. Husbands, and myself. When we absolutely did move there seemed more dispatch than had previously marked our tour; that indicated to me that we were in danger. Soon we saw the cause, as passing the works near Malvern Hill we saw our whipped Cavalry huddled behind the breastworks, both horses and riders, looking in the most perfectly exhausted condition; officer inquiring for friends, and overcasting every countenance an expression: "I hope there is *now* rest for the weary"; the horses did not look as if they could go a mile. As soon as the main road was reached we could see it was a backward move and it proved so to be. For ten miles we travelled pretty lively and parked for a few minutes, when we were ordered to load the teams upon transports and cross the James river. A scene ensued which is common upon most wharves—intensified at this time by the hunger and fatigue of the teamsters and the presence of more whiskey than regulations allow. However, a protecting power seemed extended to me as I suffered no harm in body or mind and went on board in the carriage and landed safely in a splendid sandy beach where sleep soon relieved me of all care. Mrs. Husbands was taken with an intense nervous headache and to help her with the means at my command was my desire. In the afternoon all moved to the parking ground and the tent was pitched and Mrs. Husbands safely laid upon a bed to rest and I, too, soon made, as I think, the best use of my time by going to sleep too.

June 26"—This morning is warm and still beautiful, provided you have nothing to do. It is the Sabbath day and all seem agreed to regard it as a day of rest. Mrs. Husbands is writing. The Capt. is asleep upon the beach. Mr. Wadsworth has gone somewhere and what the day may develope in regard to a movement is a question. . . . The development was this—that Dr. Douglass came down in the boat to see how we were getting along and Mrs. Husbands, much to my regret, *would* go on the boat to City Point. Here I am now established, cooking for the 1st Div. 2nd Corps Hospt. patients. Have good accomodations and good help, get along first rate. Of course, no one cares whether I have any thing or get on comfortably as they do for me when at the front but I am contented.

I would like this sent to mother and have her copy it. The first part of the march I wrote I sent to Dr. Dudley, but he will send it back and then I will send it all to you. As to ever writing another description of that battle and March! I am sick of the thoughts of it, let alone writing it out. Soldiering nowadays is hard work.

From thy sister CORNELIA

VIII
CITY POINT HOSPITAL

✿

City Point, June 26th, 1864.

MY DEAR SISTER

I AM thankful to say I am at City Point tonight all safe. I will write soon and give an account of our trip, but for fear you might have had some concern for me I write this night. Our Cavalry were badly whipped and I was in the retreat and had a pretty hard time, but am well, thanks to Providence. Gen. Grant's Head Qtrs. are in sight.

thine in haste

CORNELIA HANCOCK

It is reported at City Point I was wounded at White House.

June 27th/64 City Point.

MY DEAR MOTHER

I FEEL once more settled. I arrived here last evening after a very tedious overland route and have my tent up, stove going, and live something like I did last winter. I was in the fight at White House, of which there is a meagre account in the paper, there being but one reporter on the ground and he, with the cowardly Abercombie, retired to the gun boats soon after the fighting commenced. Mrs. Harris is here, has a tent opposite mine, but inferior in arrangement. I believe I have now the confidence of more people than almost any Lady in the army. The piece in the paper has made a great stir and gained me many enemies. I have so many friends I don't know what to do. I do, too, though, and that is to a straightforward duty and care for no one. There never was a place where you have stronger friends or more violent enemies. Miss Willetts still stays here. The weather is intensely hot, the suffering intensely great, and that I am well and happy is a great satisfaction. I received a letter from William, was very glad, but do not still know what Regt. he is in. I rec'd the Standard from thee. It is evening now. We have had scarcely one drop of rain for two weeks, the dust is shoe top deep, and the flies are almost ready to blow one while they are still alive. I have 3 men detailed for service for me and I look forward to having our men more comfortable than they are now. The Sanitary Commission is flooded with delegates and some of them of a very inferior character, then again some of the noblest souls that ever drew breath. Dr. Douglass is head of affairs, is a strong friend and Capt. Harris the most efficient agent, is more of a friend than I even care he should be. Dr. Dudley has charge of the ambulance train now and will have the Div. hospital next winter. He wants to engage me to stay in it next winter, but I tell him I will not leave Dr. Potter, nor neither would I interfere with Mrs. Lee's prerogative. She is here but I think nearly played out; she has worked harder than any galley slave I ever saw. I would like to have some of Father's nice fish. I get very tired of the army fare, it is so very monotonous. Tell Father that on the march we were reduced to hard tack and uncooked pork and I actually ate it with a keen relish. I saw Mr. Murphy of Salem in the hospital. I would like this cruel war to get over, then I could come home.

thy affectionate daughter
CORNELIA

June 29th, 1864.

MY DEAR MOTHER

I RECEIVED two letters from thee directed in Dr. Potter's care and all were forwarded from White House, so I am quite up in the world. The very best way for me to receive letters from thee is thru Dr. Potter, as he is one of the fixed planets in the army so long as the bullets do not disturb him. I am well situated, have a large tent to live in all to myself and a fly to cook in, have four men to work for me and 180 men in hospt to look after. I work all day long and at night fall right down and sleep. My capacity to sleep is fast developing in the manner father does; it is a wise provision that I can. Dr. Potter sent a Barouche, two horses and one of the Doctors down for me to come up to the front and stay at their hospt. It was a great temptation for me to go but I had just got established here and it seemed changeable to leave so soon, so I am here yet. Gen. Grant's Head Qts. are within a mile of this place. I think I will give him a call and see if he will not give me an order to go on a march with the hospt. and stay at the front all the time. The cannonading is perfectly deafening even at this distance today. It seems almost sometimes as if I could not bear it any longer. I have plenty of stores, send things up to the rifle pits to persons I know. The Sanitary are great friends of mine. I have travelled in this train so long I am well known. Having been in the White House shelling has made me very conspicuous. All I have to do is to sit down and write an order for any thing and it comes to me.

It is night now. I am sitting on my bed writing this. The boys are sitting round talking.

City Point, July 1st, 1864.

MY DEAR SISTER

I RECEIVE all your letters now regularly and think you might venture a package containing two pieces of black skirt braid, two new aprons, some clean ruffles, some sewing tackle. Our Corps has been somewhat relieved and we have fewer in hospt. as they are sent on hospt. transports as fast as possible. Miss Willetts has gone to Washington. I do not know whether she intends to return or not. I think Mrs. Lee will come home soon. She has worked very hard indeed. So has every one. We have had as high as ten thousand here at one time. Gettysburg was a skirmish comparatively speaking. The cannonading was most severe last night and it seems sickening when you know what a scene it must bring to us. I have a good cook, plenty of stores. Some are down upon the Sanitary Com. I think it a God appointed institution, tho sometimes I think God communicates very little with some of the *agents*. It is a gigantic machine. I assure you if it was not for the sea breeze from the James River we should die here; the dust is shoe top deep, the sun just pours down, the smell is almost intolerable, and we have had no rain for nearly three weeks. Wonderful to say I am well. We have ice here plenty. The wounded have no beds, however, and clouds of dust pour over them all the while.

I hope you will write to me. I just received a long letter from Doctor Child which I shall answer. I send things up to my friends in the rifle pits. Dr. Dwinelle is *here* and Dr. Dudley has undisputed charge of 2nd Div. Hosp. There will be one man that will be sorry he said so much against my serving in the *second Div.* hosp!

CORNELIA HANCOCK

City Point

MY DEAR SISTER

I RECEIVED thy letter of Sunday last, stating thee had started my things. In thy next letter state what was the direction upon the outside the box for if it is sent by Adams Express I doubt if I get it this year. The proper direction would be Capt. Isaac Harris, U. S. Sanitary Com., 244 F. St., Washington, then it would come by express to their office and to him thru their boats. The Adams Express matter sent to City Point is immense and whenever I will get it is a question. They have not been allowed to bring second Corps matter thru at all. I suppose they think the Corps will go away somewhere. I am suffering for nothing, however, and hope the box will not be lost. Mr. Wadsworth has gone to Phila. and I hope he will call to see you.

I did receive the pictures and was much obliged for them. I am glad mother is in a comfortable frame of mind over money matters; it is just as well so to be. I shall be very pleased with my carpet and table cover and will keep them even if I have to move. Any person who can barely exist ought to think they are doing well in these warm days.

117

We have had no train in so long I cannot remember the time. Sallie Ingham writes to me quite frequently. I shall come home this fall as soon as it gets cool enough to enjoy one's self.

Mrs. Husbands is back here and stays with me at present. Capt. Harris was the man who brought me the stockings, a curious present but very valuable one.

Last Sunday morning I got up about 4 o'clock and rode up to the front, spent the day with Dr. Potter in a nice house belonging to the Rebel Gen. Dearing, a splendid house, part of the family still residing there. Dr. Dudley came over but he could not enjoy himself because we did not come over to see him. I rode up and back upon horseback. Dr. Miller took me. I had just left City Point landing when that dreadful explosion took place. I was just getting Miss Willetts off who left very sick indeed. There were many lives lost and it was a frightful affair. The war news remains the same, no one very hopeful.—Dr. Dudley was down last evening to spend the evening with me. He is well and full of life as ever, rides down and back the same evening. I was sick yesterday, but think I am very lucky to come off with one day's sickness in this warm and smelly place. It is really awful here. The cannons boom along the line almost all the while, the heat is intense and the day of the explosion it seemed like what we read about hell. Our ladies in camp are being reduced considerably by sickness and indisposition to stay. I pray for health. I can stand all other hardships but sickness.

from thy sister
CORNELIA HANCOCK

City Point, July 4, 1864.

MY DEAR MOTHER

How strange to say, but William took dinner with me today! We had a real Fourth dinner, potatoes, beef, onions, canned peach pie, and corn starch pudding. I cannot say that I was very much surprised to see him for I felt pretty sure from what I could hear that they would be called to the front. They are stationed at Bermuda Hundreds now. The firing was brisk in that direction while he was here and he seemed anxious to get back, said he had raw recruits in his company. You really must not concern now for his safety for really there has been so many lives and limbs lost that it is more fashionable to be in mourning than any other way. It was mighty pleasant to see him and I think he enjoyed his visit very much. We had ice cream here this afternoon. I introduced him to all my friends. They, of course, invited him to drink some whiskey which he refused to do which is a very rare thing in the army. Dr. Miller is here on duty now. He seemed very glad to see Will. It was by luck he found I was here. Jim Patterson saw me at City Point and I told him when he went to Trenton to tell Will where I was and he met him at Bermuda Hundreds and so he came over immediately. How very glad I was to see him. He can come over frequently if he chooses. Dr. Dudley has charge of the 2nd Div. Hospital. I receive letters from him very frequently but see him none at all as he is busy and I too. If it would rain I guess he would ride into City Point, but the dust here is just like ashes, 6 inches deep.

I received a nice letter from Sarah a few days since. I will answer it soon. Is it not sad about Henry? None of you know as well as I how terrible those Cavalry raids are. I have been in one. The exhaustion of horse and rider is perfectly awful. The weather is as hot as it can be, but there is a slight air from the James. My tent is so situated that it looks right down the James; both banks are beautiful. The cannons boom all the while but little seems accomplished. We have only a moderate number in hospital now, mostly sick. It is very convenient to send the wounded army upon transports. The army had onions for the fourth of July. I have plenty of stores to feed our men upon. Also sent some things up to the rifle pits to men I know there.

Save this picture of Gen. Hays and Barlow. They are very like them. The lead pencil mark on the map marks my journeying in Virginia. I have the pleasantest tent in the hospital. I receive my

119

letters very well now. They are making me a sofa cushion for a present, Ellen says. It is a curious present, I think, for a warlike woman, but I shall be very much gratified to have it.

Dr. Dudley says three ladies have made application to come to his hospital but he says if they come he will send them away. He wants me to promise to stay with his hospt. next winter, but I am very well satisfied with Dr. Potter and shall not change. Many contrabands are here. We expect to use them for cooks in hospital. A reporter of the press of Phila. lies very sick in the hospital.

This is the plan of the hospital. The different states have stores and agents in the first row, a broad street where they drive in, rows of hospt. tents, and mine in the centre of 1st Div.

The wounded suffer for nothing save from heat.

from thy daughter, CORNELIA HANCOCK
1st Div. 2nd Corps Hospt., City Point

City Point, July 4, 1864.

MY DEAR SISTER

TODAY is the anniversary of my starting to the army. It seems as if it had been a long lifetime since that date, so much has transpired.

120

HOSPITAL AT CITY POINT

I write this letter to say that Mrs. Husbands is going home to pay a visit. She lives at 18th St. and Spruce. I would like some of you to go and see her. She can tell you everything of my performance. She was the lady who was with me on the march. If she is coming back she would bring my riding dress with her and the other things I mentioned, aprons, black braid and sewing tackle. Sanitary stuff is very plenty and the hospital is well supplied. There are very few wounded left here now, mostly sick. What is the reason I am always lucky? Do the spirits know why? Twice Dr. Potter sent for me to come to the front. Somehow I did not want to go and a blessed good thing. I was rightly impressed as Mrs. Husbands received peremptory orders to leave and if I had been *there* I should surely have fared a like fate. I made one trip up safe and got no orders, but I shall keep clear of going again. Dr. Dudley sent me a note that I had better come, too, and it was a great temptation to go but I was rightly guided. I hope I shall continue my luck.

from thy sister
CORNELIA HANCOCK

City Point, Ju. 7, 1864.

MY DEAR SARAH

I RECEIVED thy letter a few days ago. If you write me a letter saying *nothing* it is a great satisfaction to me, so do not fail to do so. Uncle Will is found as far as *I* am concerned. He took dinner with me on the 4th of July. He is at Bermuda Hundreds. I am glad they are alive at Greenwich for it seems hardly necessary that the whole world should go into mourning over this war. I want one of thy photographs very much. I will not promise but that I may lose it as I had the misfortune to lose all that were in that photograph album while I was on the march. Aunt Ellen need not think I will get killed for I have no idea of it whatever myself. Where has Charles P. Smith seen me that he should so comment? William Bradway is a great while finding out that I can do more than most women. I could have told him that long ago. Abbe Paul, no *other* Paul, must be informed how I get my clothes; it is none of *their* business.

I am glad if the piece must be published that a man of some sense wrote it. I think it an admirable piece of composition, independent of its having any reference to me. I am sorry James Hancock fell off the tree. He had better lost his life in the *army;* that is more popular at present. I would like to hear from Isabelle & Sallie Ingham very much. Miss Rebecca was exactly in her right place when she was receiving Mrs. Lincoln.

How do they take Henry's being lost. He is most probably dead.

We have just had a few drops of rain. I wish we could have more. We shall die of breathing dust. Certainly that piece upon Gen. Hays was not sent because it was *good!* Mrs. Swisshelm is most too severe, but there is truth in her assertion, too. Today one of Sheridan's cavalry gave me a very nice small mule. I took a ride upon him and he is splendid. Went to City Point with Dr. Miller. I have two side saddles in my possession now. I wish I could have him home. I think it would benefit thee to ride. We have very few in the hospital now and I have lots of help, there are floods of contrabands coming in; I have a jewel of a little boy to run my errands. I think I shall keep him while I stay for he is very useful. I am going to write a letter for the perusal of the Society, showing the operation of the Sanitary for the relief of soldiers. Mrs. Swisshelm makes this comment upon Miss Dix: "Is a self sealing can of horror tied up with red tape." Miss Dix' nurses are like all others in my estimation, some excellent, some good, some positively bad. So it would be, let who *would* have charge.

I went, day before yesterday, out 6 miles with Anna Etheridge to see some sick in the first Michigan cavalry. I rode on horse back up hills and down dale over ditches, &c. I shall soon be all right on horse back and it is very convenient here as ambulances are difficult to obtain and horses very plenty. I received a letter from mother dated July 2nd. I shall answer it soon. In it was the piece upon Lieut. Fogg, but it did not come up to my expectation. Nothing in print will ever meet my expectation on his instantaneous departure. There has not been a man lost in all my knowledge of finer promise than he. Everyone admits it. The cannonading is incessant here, but very few are wounded by it. We have plenty of water forced up by the engine from James River. The Rebels are making their summer pic-nic into Maryland. I should not be surprised if our Corps had to go up to fight them. I shall be very sorry as every one dreads the long march so much. Grant walks round the hospt. quite frequently. We have everything in the hospital heart can wish for; had splendid light cake for breakfast. I am noted all over our Div. for making good biscuit. I would like very much to have more of Ruth's leven.

I have more patients in now and have considerable to attend to.

from thy affectionate aunt

CORNELIA HANCOCK

City Point, July 10th, 1864.

MY DEAR MOTHER

I RECEIVED a short letter from thee yesterday. You certainly have had some later intelligence from me by this time. You even do not seem to know that I was in the shelling at White House. It certainly is wonderful that we live, it is so dry, but the air off the river is very bracing and we have a Christian Com. engine and hose which keeps the dust down some. But thanks to a kind providence, it is raining now copiously on the top of my tent. I hope it will continue twenty four hours. I hope Sarah Smith will get along well. If I was home I would be a good nurse, as I guess I have seen more broken legs than any other woman in Salem Co. I hope Beulah will receive the letter I sent her. How does she take William's departure? He is well as far as I know, is in the 10th Army Corps, third Div. under Butler. I would have been glad if he had joined our Corps, but being an officer he could be brought to our hospital or I could go to him. I guess he is not three miles from here. As soon as I get my riding dress I can easily ride over to see him.

I had a letter from Dr. Dudley tonight. He appears to think he

123

would like to visit City Point but is in charge and cannot leave. The 12 N. J. are to have new colors presented to them and I am invited to go out to see the presentation and if I can pass the guards I shall go. Mr. Wadsworth, the gentleman who brought me thru on the march, and Capt. Aaronson, N. J. state agent, are to take me. I have two contrabands helping me, one is an old lady, who is a perfect old slave; she is fixing round me now; calls me "honey," reminds me of neighbor Morris. Everything indicates here a protracted siege of Petersburg, but I hear the Rebs are making their summer tour into Penn. I think I will espouse *their* cause, they are so smart. The firing is incessant at the front now, but it appears to do very little damage. We are behind very strong intrenchments and abattis here. I rode to City Point with Dr. Miller on horseback this evening, went past Gen. Grant's head qtrs. and saw all around. I am sorry to disobey thy injunction but really I do like to ride on horseback and do it every day. I believe it is good for my health, too. I do not go until six o'clock and the change of scene and fresh air are beneficial to me, I think. I think I enjoy myself about as well as any one round. Have everything under my control, the Sanitary Com. endorse me as one of their ladies; no one can get more of them than I can. Some of the finest men the Lord ever let live belong to the Sanitary and also some of the most worthless. I believe I told Sarah I had a mule presented to me. They make much fun of my mule here, but I take notice they borrow it quite frequently. I have turned him over to Dr. Dudley to dispose of and he will do something with it that will turn to account. I am just getting supper, farina, white Indian mush, canned peaches, toast, and tea.

The first Div. band are playing beautiful music. The leader serenaded me "the first lady on the ground"; reason, because I gave him his dinner! He has a piece called the Hancock Gallop, which is beautiful.

July 14th—My letters become very much soiled lying round; there is no news here. No one is excited about the Rebs. going into Maryland; an old soldier just as leave fight one spot as another and they

124

are in hopes the northern people will be disturbed; the feeling is a sort of spite against those who have never been in the war.

I hear William's Regt. has been sent to Maryland but do not tell it as truth. I have seen him but the once and have heard nothing direct from him since.

from thy daughter

C. HANCOCK

City Point Hospt, 1st Div. 2nd Corps
July 14, 1864.

MY DEAR SISTER

I RECEIVED a letter dated July 2nd from thee. I receive very few letters from any source except from Surg. at the front. I do not know whether you write few or whether I do not get them. Do you get letters from me? I could tell Mr. Owen many an interesting tale if I live to see him again. Glory to the Fair. We feel the effects of it here. At least we feel the effects of *something* as we have plenty to eat and drink. Mrs. Swisshelm nor no other person ought to have the *direction* of nurses. Not one woman in ten thousand is fit to have one might of authority. Mrs. Swisshelm would be the best of any person I know, but there is no need of any one, there is enough will volunteer. We have more here this minute than are employed. I sent the diary I kept on the march up to the front to convince them I was not wounded. I am thankful I was not scared to death and also that I was not wounded. It has been just one sea of misery here all summer and I suppose the Philada hospt. are dreadful now with convalescents. The Salem people do not write me at all now. I do not know but they have given me over for a reprobate entirely.

William is all right at Bermuda Hundreds. Miss Willetts' brother is in the same Regt. a Seargt. He is visiting here today. I could easily ride out to where they are on horseback, but I do not believe William cares for me to come. He can come here as often as he wishes to see me.

125

I do not wish to hear about Rylands campaign; do not take thy time writing about it. Capt. Harris was a graduate of Antioch College and knows Henry Warriner. I cannot tell how sorry I am about Henry. Poor fellow, I know by sad experience how he felt. I saw them fall by the roadside in Sheridan's raid and had I not been in a wagon myself should have fallen out, too. There is no use in making any acct. of it however, for it is the common lot of soldiers.

All suffer this campaign. I have lost all interest in political affairs, have no eyes, ears, for anything but the sufferings of the soldiery. We have now a splendid hospital and everything to make the men comfortable. I am well, take a ride on horseback every night, get a letter from Dr. Dudley twice a week. Have everything my own way. Dr. Hammond, our Div. Surg. thinks I am just right and I get along very well. The Rebs. are making their summer pic-nic. I have faith to believe we will go into winter quarters at Brandy Sta. or perhaps a trifle nearer Washington, there spend the winter, and look forward to a glorious spring campaign in which the Rebels will all be starved to death and utterly be annihilated from the face of the earth. God grant it might be so. But U. S. Grant knows better, that it will not be so. I shall be out of stockings soon. I am low in the dress line, too. I would like to have a green or blue plaid gingham made so it could be sent if an opportunity offered. Care of Sanitary Commission, care of Dr. Douglass, would probably be the best way to send any thing. Did thee ever go to see Mrs. Husbands, 18th & Spruce? I wrote thee to do so. My gingham dresses have done well, I assure thee; look nicely yet.

Send me a ruffle and a small meshed black silk net, small sized, in a letter. Colored soldiers are all round. Miss Gillson, a young lady who has been in the army a long time, is with their hospital. Tell Doctor I inquired for Albert Ricker. He has been sent to a Genl. hospt. North somewhere. He was at City Point sick. I would have been glad to have done anything for him if I could have seen him.

Dr. Roland was here to dinner today. Everybody comes down but Dr. Dudley. He has charge of the Div. hospt. and cannot leave.

He says he will pretend sick and come. I have a contraband woman to work for me. She does very well, stays with me at night, and sleeps in as good a bed as I do, much to the astonishment of the other ladies of the camp.

Mr. Wadsworth has offered $5. reward for my photograph Album and says he knows it is in the San. Com. train. Capt. Harris is home in Brooklyn. I hope I may get my album again. I thought so much of it.

I want my dress to have braid around the bottom. It keeps them together much longer. I have ten $ but it would not be safe to send it at this time.

Thy sister
CORNELIA

City Point, 1st Div. 2nd Corps Hospital
July 18th, 1864.

To Joanna Dickeson, Pres. of
Ladies Aid, Hancock's Bridge,
Salem Co., N. J.

MY DEAR FRIENDS:

THINKING you might like to hear a little of hospital life as I see it manifested here, I now address you. At Fredericksburg we received the wounded from the Wilderness. There was more suffering there for want of food than I ever witnessed anywhere. From Fredericksburg we went to Port Royal. Had the base of operations there for a short time only when all moved to White House. There the wounded were brought from the fight upon the North Anna River and it was another dreadful scene. I joined the train which had been three days coming from the field having had no attention except what could be given to them lying in the ambulances. All expected to be relieved from their unpleasant situation; but when we got to the Pamunkey River the bridge was destroyed so we could not cross and soon we saw that another day of trial was before the wounded.

127

I was with the San. Com. train and in the wagon were stores plenty. Mrs. Lee in company with me cooked them a bountiful meal and I took water from the river and washed the face and hands of all in our Div. train. To wash one's face and hands when on duty is considered a luxury at any time, but no one can know the relief one feels in using water after a three days' march, especially when wounded. Some men you could hardly recognize if you knew them intimately.

There has been no day's work that I have done since this campaign that gave such extreme relief as cleansing those poor fellows' faces. All were cases of severe wounds. At dark night while it was raining the long train moved over a newly constructed bridge and loaded the men in transports. In the second Corps hospital the wounded continued rapidly to arrive until they laid out in the open field without any shelter. Here I dressed more wounds than in all my experience before. There were not surgeons near enough who were willing to stay in the sun and attend to the men and it was too awful to leave them uncared for. Just for one moment consider a slivered arm having been left three days, without dressing and the person having ridden in an army wagon for two days with very little food. They mostly arrived at night when all the ladies would fill their stores and feed them as they came in. They would then remain in the ambulance until morning when probably no shelter could be procured for them and here they lay in the scorching sun during 1/2 the day. It was at this time there was such crying need to dress their wounds, some of which had not been opened for 36 hours. Such tired, agonized expressions no pen can describe. By the time one set of men were got in and got comfortable another set would arrive, and so it continued night and day for about two weeks. At that time there was a very good opportunity to make a visit to the hospital up at the extreme front. There I stayed for a week, the men were then in the rifle-pits and if they moved out to get a drink of water were shot in the action. I saw them as soon as they were wounded but the custom is here to operate upon the wound and immediately send them to

128

the rear. So there is very little opportunity for a lady to be of much service. When the Hospt. was ordered to move I came back to White House and found all wounded removed and the place ready to be evacuated. I remained behind to go thru with the Sanitary Com. train, thinking to get to the James River ahead of those going round in transports, but was very much mistaken in that. As we were dependent upon Sheridan cavalry for an escort they were detained fighting for one week. And a long, tiresome week of waiting was before us. But the monotony was broken upon the 20th of June by the Rebels planting a battery upon a hill and shelling our train for six hours, in which time it behooved all to make the best of the situation and keep out of the shells as best we could. One shell struck in the rear of the carriage I was in and one rifled cannon came between Mrs. Husbands and myself while we were walking along the beach. However, suffice it to say no lives were lost in our train except three horses; a wagon also was destroyed. After the shelling commenced the train passed to the south side of the Pamunkey River and there remained until Sheridan and his cavalry returned and then started for City Point, having only one encounter with the Rebs on the way. The most intense suffering of the wounded at the assault on Petersburg was passed by the time I arrived at City Point, and the hospital now bears the appearance of a General Post hospital. The different states have agencies here whose tents are in a row at the head of the hospital. Then the tents stretch in long rows about one half mile, the ladies' cooking tents are between the rows, the front of mine is on the main street facing the agencies, and the rear is used to give food from to the respective nurses of the wards. Our sick are magnificently supplied in hospt. now. Twice have I given ice cream to my patients. There is in every hospt. a fund which accrues from the sick not using all their legal rations which, if properly managed, supplies the sick with many luxuries. Then there is the Medical Purveyor, another source for delicacies; then all deficiencies are supplied by Sanitary and Christian Com. The mode the Sanitary operates is this—they bring a large stock of food on barges which lay at City Point. Then in every Corps they put a large tent and stores are sent to it; then every lady who has charge of a cooking tent makes out a requisition for what she needs and sends it to this Sanitary tent and there the requisition is filled excepting liquors which cannot be drawn except on a Surgeon's order. Then besides this, in every section there is an agent who visits the tents, supplies the men with clothing, tobacco, pipes, &c. The Christian Com. I do not think as well organized, at least they have a different organization. They generally pitch a large tent and cook their own food and distribute it thru their own agents, which is done in a desultory and fitful manner which disturbs the good order of the hospital and frequently Surgeons forbid their coming into the wards. They prefer the victuals should be dealt out with regularity from regularly established cook kitchens. The time the Christian Com. do great service is right after battle, then their pails of punca and kettles of farina, even if not prepared in the very best manner, are very good for starving men. The Sanitary have feeding stations, too, at all wharves and depots for wounded. Of course, in large bodies of people like the agents of either Com. you will find ungentlemanly and unprincipled men, but the good that either commission does can never be estimated. We have water forced from the river by engines, so water is plenty. Everything is plenty and if our soldiers could only commence to see the end of this war they would be happy and even jubilant. But they are not at this time especially jubilant. We have only sick now here and they are very different from wounded as they many of them have been sick and exposed for a long time. This is especially written for the perusal of those who still attend the sewing circle for the benefit of soldiers.

From CORNELIA HANCOCK

City Point, July 20th, 1864.

MY DEAR MOTHER

I RECEIVED a letter from thee dated July 14th. I am glad you are so attentive to Beulah, it almost seems as if you ought to live together,

130

your families are so reduced by war. I hope Mary had good success with her pic-nic. To look back it seems strange that I should have ever taken such a lively interest in engineering one as I did a few years ago. It is very dry here, but there is so much water forced up from the river that we do not feel it as we would have. It has rained too, some. Henry's being a prisoner would be a very sorrowful thing to me if I was home, but here I am so accustomed to hear of first one person I know and another being captured that it does not impress me as if I was out of this miserable place. Capt. Derickson on Genl. Barlow's staff, was captured on the 22nd of June, a splendid young man. I have his photograph. If I look as if I was ninety when I get home you need not be surprised, for something has happened to almost all I ever knew. Gen. Barlow spent about one half hour in my quarters today. He is a man of very few words and *he* complimented very highly upon my establishment. Bridget, who lives with me, was very much delighted to think her floor was scrubbed. She is a woman who has been in the army for three years, done all the marching with the regt. and is a splendid hand to work.

Dr. Dudley came from the front and spent last Sunday with me. He is the most sensible young man I ever knew. He has never left the front before during this campaign. I suppose if William is wounded he would have himself brought here or I would go to him. I just received a long and interesting letter from Ellen. She is in Salem, I perceive. I mailed a letter to your Ladies Aid Society.

Today I am having my tent re-rigged and an addition thereto. Soldiers work so slowly that I have sat down in despair of ever getting thru. It will be nice tho when finished. A dining room, sleeping apartment and kitchen. Tell Ellen if she has an opportunity to send my things by the N. J. agent it will be the very plan, and if she can put in anything gay like a carpet or such like to fix up my quarters, so much the better. They will come free of expense, too. Let Isabella send me something like a tablecloth or something fancy. We have not had a battle in so long that we are becoming quite civilized in our mode of living. Anything that is pretty I would like to see. I

131

wish instead of the cushion the ladies of Ellen's friends had sent me a nice carpet. Impress it upon Ellen's mind that thru that N. J. agency things will be safe for me.

The tent is up today and I am getting fixed up very nicely, indeed. I wish you could see me. I think Grant is going to make a regular siege of Petersburg. If so, it is as well that we should get fixed as nicely as possible. We soon begin to look homelike in camp if left still for any length of time. I had some splendid ice cream at my quarters last evening and Dr. Dougherty and staff spent the evening with me. He is medical inspector of the 2nd Army Corps. I have seen all the celebrities I care to see except Gen. Hancock. I think fate is against my ever seeing him. I heard he was to be here yesterday but he did not appear.

I have everything going on this morning. I have six new tents added to my care now as Mrs. Lee leaves in a few days. I hope to hear from you soon. I will answer Ellen's letter.

from thy daughter

CORNELIA

William is well and safe for the present.

City Point, 1st Div. 2nd Corps. Hospt.
July 23rd, 1864.

MY DEAR SISTER

I RECEIVED a long and interesting letter from thee while at Salem. My things will be perfectly safe in the N. J. agent's hands. Lizzie's and thy representation differ in regard to Dr. Aiken's visit. Dr. Aiken is a loss to the service. He was a kind and good man to *all* suffering soldiers. He was a great friend to Mrs. Lee and tried to have Dr. Dudley promise to send for her to come to the hospital next winter. He does not like her and would not do it. He still insists upon not having a woman in his hospital and says because he found me a single exception it does not prove his rule is bad. I think he is wrong, but it is somewhat difficult to convince him.

132

I had a lieut. from Will's company to dinner today. William is well and if they could get enough to eat they would be doing extremely well. This is a beautiful Sabbath day. I think thee would give $5. to spend this day here. My place now is simply magnificent, the view is right down the James River. I have two hospital tents, well floored, and a large fly tent to cook in, two iron bedsteads with white linen sheets, and four good chairs; that red thing Aunt Hannah gave me is strung up to look fancy. I have two hundred to look after the low diet; have an Irish woman, one contraband woman, and boy, and one soldier. I have a first rate work squad and my quarters are by all allowed to be the best in the army hospitals hereabouts. My things will be safe in the N. J. agent's care (Capt. Aaronson). In all coming time you can send a box to Trenton and have it forwarded free to me in that channel. I received a letter from Mother today.

Did I ever tell thee I had a little mule presented to me. Dr. Dudley would not countenance the mule at all. I told William he might have it if he wanted it to draw the water for the company. Of course he wanted it and Lieut. Munn took it over yesterday. They are about eight miles from here. Dr. Dudley says I can have one of his horses to keep, but I must *not* ride a *mule*.

Today is the first day I have felt at all encouraged about the war news. Some reliable friends of mine were down from the front and say they are actually undermining the forts rapidly around Petersburg. Maybe Grant knows what he is at.

I went down to City Point on a swift horse last evening. You need not think I am in any danger from rebels here for it is not so. Mother seems afraid to have me ride on horse back. Any person who practices as much as I do, it is extremely difficult to find a horse in the army with enough spirit to throw you. Dr. Dudley has offered to send me down a horse for me to keep here all the while but I declined the offer. He was here on Sunday last and he and Dr. Miller took me the nicest ride I have had. I had Dr. Dudley's best horse and there is a great difference in horses gaits, as to whether they are easy or not.

There is very little that happens new and strange here, so I have nothing more to say.

from thy sister

CORNELIA HANCOCK

City Point, August 15, 1864.

MY DEAR MOTHER

I HAVE just received thy letter dated the 9th. Ellen says she has dispatched the box. I have not received it yet, but hope to soon. Thee could not have made a more apt contribution than the skirt for I have lost, in the most mysterious manner, one of mine. I believe Aunt Hannah contributed a table cloth and piece of carpet. I shall enjoy them very much if I ever receive them. We have had no wounded for some time now, but are expecting them fully today. The Corps has been in action yesterday near Ft. Darling. On the 11th orders were received for the Corps to come to City Point and be shipped in transports with out any destination assigned them. They were all jubilant thinking they were going to Washington. I never spent such a day in the army. Every person who ever knew me called here as they passed, and *they* could be counted by hundreds. Capt. Acton and Maj. Chew took breakfast with me. Dr. Dudley rode ahead of the column and was first man here. His Col. has been made Brig. Gen. and they, with Dr. Maull, were the last to leave. Three of the nicest men in the army. No one could possibly have received more attention than I did during the 15 hours the Corps remained in our vicinity. Heartfelt attention, too. Men that I have helped in distress and all kinds of men. I saw everybody I wanted to but Elisha Stewart, and his natural want of energy was all that hindered him from coming here. Lots of his Regt. were here. He is well, I heard from him. E. Powell nor R. Seeley know very little what they are talking about, and any person who says a word against a soldier who has endured this campaign will have a black line marked against them thru all eternity. No one knows what all of us suffer here and I hope they

134

never will know. But there is one thing I would like them to know that God will never prosper them in anything while they talk so. They cannot hurt thee or thine for thee owns two as cheerful soldiers as were ever in the Union army. William was here all day yesterday, a perfect embodiment of self-complacency and satisfaction. He comes over every other Sunday, has his good dinner and long nap. They are having very light soldiering, if it only continues. No marching. But it is liable to change any moment. This country is all alive with cannon, you can hear them firing everywhere round. I am very tired of the sound. I hope Sally and Lizzie will not laugh immoderately, but tell father in these war times laughing is but a small matter. I would like to see our children, all of them. My coming home is very uncertain. William wants me to come when he does. Dr. Dudley wants to get a leave of absence when I am home so I do not know yet. Nor can we tell a day ahead here what we ought to do. I do not care how much it cost to come home, I am coming when I get ready.

I have very comfortable quarters and if I don't feel like work do not have to do it, but have a great deal of care, 183 low diet patients. If I am sick Bridgett takes excellent care of me and gets along very well. Give my love to all the family.

from thy daughter

CORNELIA HANCOCK

August 17, 1864.

MY DEAR SISTER

I RECEIVED thy note by Mr. Wadsworth and you may well know I was delighted to see him back having seen you all. Is he not a pleasant man? He enjoyed his visit immensely. Poor Dr. Dudley has given out at last. He went on the last raid with the second Corps in high spirits thinking they were going to Washington and make a raid thru Maryland, but they were doomed to disappointment. They only went to Deep Bottom and into a fight on that awful hot day, last Sunday. The Dr. gave out on Sunday night, was almost sunstruck.

Said he was hard sick, was on a stretcher, and should come down to this hospital if he did not get better soon. I look for him down tonight. Gen. Barlow is here played out. Why are they not all played out? The cannons are belching forth with double venom tonight, I hope to some effect. We have been repulsed and driven so far as Deep Bottom. Capt Dod who was in Henry's company, is here sick. He asked for me as soon as he came and when he is able he takes his meals in my tent. Thee need not be concerned about opening my letters at all. *My orders are to open all you want to of them.* I am not ashamed of any correspondence I have.

I am going to have Indian cakes for supper. Our hospital is again filled with wounded. The ground is literally covered with sick and wounded. I have been the whole length of the line and the cook house is full, on the table, under the table—everywhere. It is raining tonight which is refreshing to us all. But makes it bad travelling. Dr. Dudley is better and is at his post yet. Dr. Aiken came in very unexpectedly last evening. He will be detailed to stay with us, I think. I hope so.

There are, of course, many disagreeable reports circulated by those who have various motives for circulating them, some of which may reach you, but you can rely on my doing my straight forward duty at all times and all reports that arise come of my off hand manner that by some are misconstrued. I have as good a time as any one and everything in this world goes by comparisons. This morning five doctors, whose time was out, asked the privilege of taking breakfast with me and said their last association with the army would be rememberances of me. Dr. Houston, Surg. in-chief of the 1st Div., was one of them. He lives second and Pine. Said maybe he would call to see you. Maybe Dr. Child will go to see him. The air is perfect here this morning. We need rain very much. Everyone is expecting a terrible battle. I feel very well today, very little work to do.

from thy sister

CORNELIA HANCOCK

August 21st, 1864.

MY DEAR MOTHER

I RECEIVED a note from thee expressive of concern for my health. I am very careful, indeed have to be in this place or would be sick. Dr. Dudley is here, very ill with fever. Dr. Miller has him in his tent and we are doing everything we can for him. An order came for a dead man to be dug up and recognized and Dr. Dudley was the only man in the hospital who knew him. So this afternoon we had to put him in an ambulance and carry him to the ground, open the grave, and he had to examine the body. It was a disagreeable task for a well man and it like to have finished *him*. He is worse in consequence this evening. But he is a strong man and I hope will be better soon. We have 2200 men in hospital. Sickness is the order of the day here but I have been preserved so far. And I hope I will be.

Dr. Miller's wife is here and we have plenty of help to take care of Dudley. He is so very sick he is not much trouble now. Capt. Dod of Henry's company is now on Gen. Hancock's staff and is here quite sick. He asked for me as soon as he came. I wrote for his mother to come to him.

I do not feel much like writing to night.

from thy daughter, CORNELIA HANCOCK

I have not heard from Will for a week. There has been some fighting by the tenth Corps but I guess not his portion. I take it he is all right or I should hear from him. It is only about three miles from here.

[From Capt. Charles Dod to his Mother]

1st Div. 2nd Corps Hospital
City Point, Aug. 17th, 1864.

DEAREST MOTHER

I CAME here day before yesterday. I was so much under the influence of opium and quinine and suffering so much pain that I

137

could not write. Today I feel a little better but I fear will be sick longer than I expected. Yesterday I saw a lady about 21 or 22 years old, well dressed and very pretty, coming into the ward. What was my surprise to hear her inquiring if Capt. Dod was here. Although lying on my cot in terrible dishabille, I signified that I was the gentleman wanted. It turned out to be Miss Hancock, cousin of Henry Smith's and Morris Stratton's. She said she felt as if she had known me for a long time and was very glad of an opportunity of serving me. Without my knowing it she solicited permission from Dr. Hammond to let me take my meals with her. So at every meal time she sends an orderly who when I am well enough carries me down. She is constantly sending me little delicacies and I feel that it is almost worth while to be sick to obtain such treatment. She is well known, and as much loved in the 2nd Corps as Florence Nightingale was in the British Army. I have the dysentery but not a bad case of it.

Ever your loving son, CHARLIE

P. S. Dr. Hammond has just been in and says that I also have intermittent symptoms and prescribed accordingly. Please don't worry or think of coming down until I stop writing.

———————

Aug. 22, 1864.

MY DEAR MOTHER

I WROTE to thee last night but since then heard William was sick and have been over to see him, and for fear you may have heard that he is sick I write to say he has merely an attack of intermittent fever and I hope will be better soon. If he is sick three days longer he is coming over to stay with me where he can have as good and better medical care than at home and everything necessary to make him comfortable. Dr. Dudley is much the same as when last I wrote. I am well.

from thy daughter, C. HANCOCK

I will write you all the time while Will is sick.

138

City Point, Aug. 27, 1864.

MY DEAR SISTER

EVENTS have passed in such rapid succession before us for the past few days I do not know whether I have acknowledged the receipt of the box or not. I did receive it all right and the things were nice. The dress beautiful. Our Corps has gone again "once more to the breach." And in the *papers* with *"glorious success"* I suppose, but *here* where the truth is known, death, disaster, and retreat; but killing lots of Rebels. Capt. Dod is now dying in my bed. He got up out of his bed and came up here and was too sick to be taken back. His mother came last night. It is a deathbed just like a home deathbed and is very affecting. Dr. Dudley is better, was determined to go to City Point yesterday. Then when he returned the officers of his Regt. came in wounded from the front. He got up reeling from side to side of the walk and went to every one. I went with him and the bloody fellows looked in better condition than he himself. This morning he is up and at them again and is exhausted and gone to sleep. It is a privilege all enjoy—to kill themselves—and he is trying it. Col. Thompson of the 12th N. J. is severely wounded. Lieut. Stratton killed &c. Oh! what a sight it is to see them. Miller & Dudley and myself did all we could for them. The Asst. Surg. of Dudley's Regt. had his head badly wounded by shell. I do not know when I wrote last nor what I wrote, but am thousand times obliged for Box and shoes, very opportune both.

from thy sister, C. HANCOCK

I am well. Miss Willetts is better, I hear. Allan Hoxie was shot with 5 bulletts—is dead.

Aug. 27th, 1864.

MY DEAR MOTHER

I HARDLY know when last I wrote or what I wrote, but I hardly suppose it possible to write too often.

Capt. Dod of Henry's company, died in my bed today. His mother arrived in time to see him just one day and night. He sent

139

for me to come to him in the wards and after he became very ill, in his delirium, he came to my tent and I kept him as long as he lived. He is the first man I ever saw who was fixed up nicely, like as if he was at home. The scene was very affecting and I shall never forget it. His mother took his pocket book from his pocket and gave me all that was in it which she said she knew was the wish of her son ($100). I did not want to take it but she said she intended to give all his pay to the Sanitary Com. and she wanted me to take that and buy a remembrance of him and give what I chose to the soldiers. So I have the money and shall check fifty to the Dr. to keep until such time as I have a house of my own and then buy something nice with it, marked with the event of Capt. Charles H. Dod's death. The other $50. I shall give to soldiers as occasion arises. He was a splendid looking officer and died a Christian death. He put all his dependence upon my energies in this world and the Savior for the next. Aug. 27th was the date of Capt. Charles H. Dod's death (Please preserve this letter for me, mother).

William is much better. Dr. Clark was over to see us today. Dr. Dudley is better but is as headstrong about going round as it is possible for any person to be. The officers were very much cut up in his Regt. and he got up out of bed and went to see them, every one of them, and now is only middling. The Asst. Surg. of his Regt. was seriously wounded on the head. About the proportion between the two men, Dudley would have been all stove to pieces. Lt. Col. Thompson was seriously wounded. Lt. Rich also and Lieut. Stratton killed. I expect now soon to be the only Remnant of our Corps left. We were whipped *badly* in the Weldon R.R., no matter what the news.

from thy daughter, CORNELIA

City Point, Sept. 2nd, 1864.

MY DEAR SISTER

I RECEIVED a letter from thee dated Aug. 16th which took a trip up to the front before it reached me. The direction on the box was correct enough to bring it safely to me and that is the main thing. I like people to do as I tell them even if in some cases it may turn out wrong; and about things relative to army matters no one has a better chance to know than myself. The weather is now so much cooler I do not fear being sick near as much as I did. It is a great relief to know tho that you would be cared for soon by those interested in your recovery in this selfish region of country. While I am able to help others I am much account but once helpless persons would commence to wonder who Miss Hancock was. It is cool and pleasant here now. Mother and Sallie seem both to be sick and down hearted. If they keep sick thee had better go round to see them. William has been sick a few days but as soon as the Regt. moved in front of Petersburg he got well and marched with the rest. I have not seen him for a week but have heard he was well. William takes a philosophical view of things and we might as well. That we must conquer is a sure thing in time. The only thing, I like to hear the *truth* owned in the papers as we go along. When the Rebels best us acknowledge it, draft more men to make us strong to whip them *next time.*

William certainly was putting on style when he mentions "obedient." Henry is dead according to my way of thinking. I am having easy times in hosp. now. Our sick and wounded having most of them been sent away. The talk is now that all hospital arrangements are to be removed to Hampton Roads. It makes no difference to me where it is. I am inconvenienced very much by having lent my saddle to a lady in the cavalry corps who has skedaddled with it in her possession to the Shenandoah Valley. The depravity of persons in the army is beyond belief. She promised to bring it back. Mrs. Miller is very sick tonight. I was sent for after I had closed doors for the night. My quarters are admired very much, my carpet and table cloth particularly.

I have a present of something almost every day, my watch chain is full of trinkets. Today the boys gave me this piece of chain. I would like it fixed into a good chain for my watch and sent to me.

I want, in the next letter, sent me a lot (1 doz.) rings to attach trinkets of various kinds to my chain, small rings. I lost three articles off my chain the other day for which I was very sorry. I will send my ruffles home to be washed and they can come back in the letters. Bridgett wants a plain black net like mine. Mine was very nice. She will pay for it; send the price and we will pay the bill. Dr. Burmeister does not return. He must be sick I suppose. Dr. Dudley is much better and gone to his Regt. He asked to be relieved from charge of the hospt because he thought Dr. Aiken wanted the situation and he likes best to be with his Regt. The officers of his Regt. are a lot of the most jolly and good men I ever saw. In the fight at the Reams Station Capt. Hawley was killed and three Capt. wounded severely the evening they arrived at City Point; Dr. Dudley was sick in bed but he got up, came as far as my quarters, rested a while and went to see every one of them. They were all very glad to see him and absolutely hugged each other. The next day he dressed every one of their wounds. With the exception of the Maj. they seem to think a deal of each other.

Dr. Dudley has been in the service three years the 1st of this month and he has to stay a year from next April because he was transferred from one Regt. to another. He does not wish to leave the service until his Regt. is mustered out, which is a year from this Sept. He does wish to get out then and has the same right to that Dr. Aiken had. He will not do as Dr. Aiken did. He will either do one thing or the other at that time, choose the service for his profession permanently, go into the Reg. Army, or go home and stay there. He is a much more practical man than Dr. Aiken is, not so impulsive. And not as much of a politician, for which I am very thankful. He wants the war over, the Rebels well whipped, and peace to be in the land, so one can stay at home in peace and contentment. He knows he has his own mark to make in the world and must get out of the war and get at it, or stay in the war permanently and have it for a profession. I have a dim hope we can finish this war this coming winter.

142

The riding dress is very useful, the body would still fit A. E. Cook better than I, as I am much thinner than when I left home. But I just wear the skirt with the imperishable blue saque and it is all right. The gingham fits splendidly in every particular. The brown dress is about six inches too long, but there are plenty of tailors to make it shorter right in the wards handy.

Send me a clean ruffle. I have several dirty ones to send on. I am not at all for faltering nor growing weary. I would not acknowledge that it is any less our duty to whip the Rebs now we find it hard to do. But there is no use in regarding them as played out, for it is not so. Their spirit is in them yet very strong.

I read every word of the sermon and think it excellent. I have lent it now and will send it to Doctor Dudley. I would love to see the children any time. It is all right that Eddie's nose should bleed if he undertakes to be like me. Let him go the whole figure and that he could not do unless his nose bled. Mine bleeds yet. I enjoy persons sailing under their own colors and I guess Aunt Susan will keep hers flying at masthead during life—"money, money, money." What was the Col.'s name? Probably I should know him. To what Regt. did he belong? The *uniform* has no charms to me, if I could see a man in citizen rig I think I should jump for joy. Give my love to Weatherlow. I have a Seargt. of his Regt. under my care now that was wounded at Deep Bottom, and a good boy.

This morning is Sunday. Everything is clean and nice here. I would like some of my friends to be here to spend the day. I hope William will be here. My shoes did fit and came in a very opportune time. Miss Willetts talks of coming back. Abbe Gibbon was here in the place where Miss Willetts was before she came. Aunt Hannah I suppose wants Richmond taken as bad as ever.

I am very much obliged to Eddie for the flag. It lies on my center table.

from thy sister, C. HANCOCK

Dutch Gap I know less about than thee does. I only know there is no firing in that direction now and there used to be an incessant

143

one. William writes to me quite frequently. Miss Hart sends her love. To show how we enjoy ourselves—we get a bucket full of oysters and put them into the fire and roast them. Somebody is mostly in, Dr. Ribble, for instance. This is always in the evening after all the work is done. People do not know half how to live in the north or they would have open fire places. There is a prospect of being paid $16. per month. I want some Post Stamps. And I think I had better have $5. sent to me. Somehow I feel afraid to be here without any money. I have no use for it either.

from thy sister, CORNELIA HANCOCK

City Point, Sep. 4, 1864.

MY DEAR MOTHER

I AM sitting in Dr. Miller's tent. Mrs. Miller is sick. I thought maybe thee was sick and I would write to thee before I hear from thee. I always answer all letters as soon as I receive them. Dr. Dudley has gone to his Regt. Capt. Dod is dead and I am very much relieved of business. Our sick are nearly all sent to Washington. There is great talk of moving the hospital to Hampton Roads. It makes not one particle of difference to me where the hospt is. I am well. Capt. Hancock has not been heard from for a week but he is all right or he would have been heard from. I am back in my own quarters again now and have very little of interest to write. I received a letter from Benj. Acton thanking me for informing of Frank's safety after the fight at Reams Station.

It seems to me I write a plenty but I get very confused in my mind what I have told *you* and what I have told Ellen. The report here is that Atlanta is taken, great rejoicing among our soldiers. But the one engrossing subject now is the nomination of George B. McClellan. If it is left to the soldiers his election is sure. It really seems to me marvellous they should have such a strong feeling for him. I left this open to see if I would not hear from William, which I did. He is well and is very good about sending me word; whether it is because he wants the things I send him or to relieve me of anxiety, I do not know.

from thy daughter CORNELIA

Henry has been heard from. He is in Charleston.

City Point, Sept. 6th, 1864.

MY DEAR SISTER

I KEEP writing to you considerably, and it does not seem to me I get many letters, but never blame any one for I never know whether I get all that are sent to this uncertain country. I had one section in the hospt. taken away and another given to me; the old one ate one meal at their new hotel and petitioned to come back and the Dr. granted it and now I have three sections. It is too much. They do everything for me that is possible, offer me more help, anything. But I cannot wield but a certain amount of help; more is a burden to me, the head work must proceed from me. I received a letter from thee dated Sept 4th. A box came for Capt. Dod. I had an order to open it and found nice eatables, a box of cigars and a lot of fine smoking tobacco, all of which is very readily disposed of here.

Rain will stop military operations whenever it continues any length of time. I had always thought Henry was dead. I wish Capt. Dod was living that I could tell him of his being yet alive. I am glad Emily Howland is home; anybody is a great deal better off at home if they are only contented. But I know I should not be so if I was there. I know no more about whether Mary Reed ought to have that garret room than an Egyptian mummy. I feel that it has been so long since I saw that Garret room that I hardly know whether I would give it up to Mary R. or not. It is bad that John does not turn to some *business*. It seems to me a very poor time to commence a profession at this time when there is so much disturbance in the country and so little prospect of settled professional habits. Some office in regard to the war would be a good thing. Is not Lizzie going on at Miss Margaret's? There is no use, however,

145

in looking ahead a day in these times for the Rebs. are coming in our rear and they may take all responsibility of action from us. I am rejoiced over the taking of Atlanta. Many in the army think Richmond must fall before election. But what is exasperating is the great exuberance of joy among the soldiers at the nomination of McClellan. It seems so stupid in them to me; after all they have suffered, to go back to Mc.C. William is lying up in the breastworks all right. Sends down to me for grub. He is well. Dr. Dudley did not succeed in killing himself, has gone to his Regt. and says he is living with a truly Christian man which is very pleasant, only that he feels the contrast so very great.

Sep. 9, 1864.

MY DEAR MOTHER

WILLIAM was here to spend the day yesterday, looks first rate. They are in the breastworks around Petersburg now. He said it was a great relief to lie down where you were certain to wake up without having been shot. But after our soldiers are as worn out as they get, sometimes it does not make any difference; if they are shot they do not wake up. A Lieut. had a ball enter his shoulder and it embedded itself under the shoulder blade and he never waked up at all. This you cannot believe in Jersey but if you lived here you would. I have seen with my own eyes things as remarkable, and have even experienced the amount of exhaustion that is necessary, to be shot and *not feel it*. On the march that is the one experience that above all was hard to bear personally. Our Corps is now way off on the Weldon R.R. expecting hard fighting every day.

Dr. Dudley is with his Regt. now. I should not be surprised if he were wounded or killed. He is not a shirk nor a *dead beat*— and there is very little show for a brave man's life in this campaign.

I think Sarah must certainly have forgotten she has an Aunt Nellie. I am going to send her the buttons she wanted. They were taken from Capt. Conway's vest; he was shot thru the lungs and died.

146

When Capt. Harris comes down I will get him to send the box, it will be about two inches square and I guess it can be mailed. I have a man to call upon for almost every errand and Cap. Harris will do anything for me. Did you ever get his picture. I sent it in a letter. He is a splendid man. He is Superintendant of the Sanitary Com. at the front. Did you get the description of Capt. Dod's death and save the same?

I am perfectly well since the weather has got cooler. It does not rain here yet of any account. I hope you are not sick that you do not write. Mrs. Miller is here quite sick. I think she will have to return home.

Dr. Parmer says to say in this that he has given me a most beautiful peach. Sutlers have very nice peaches here; sometimes they are distributed, too, thru the hospital quite plentifully by the Christian and Sanitary Com. How is your society flourishing?

There is nothing new in the military world except Atlanta is taken. We are very glad of that I hope to get a letter from you soon.

from thy daughter, CORNELIA HANCOCK

Sep. 11, 1864.

MY DEAR MOTHER

TODAY the wife of one of the soldiers died and he wanted very much to go home. I took his telegram to the Surg. and he said he would have to forward his request to Gen. Hancock and await his decision. The soldier started with a heavy heart to the front to try his luck, got two miles and commenced raising blood, so that he had to come back. I was advised by several surg here to go to Gen. Grant and get a furlough direct. No military man could go because it was *informal* and would not be granted. They all had faith in my ability to obtain it, and sent me an ambulance to go and try. I went and had a short interview with Grant's Adjutant Gen. and in two hours time a furlough was in the soldier's hands for 20 days.

147

My fame has spread the length and breadth of this camp. Such a miracle accomplished in so short a time. All who know me say it is easier to grant my request than to undertake to deny me because I am so persevering. That remark was made to Albert Dod. He asked if my requests were not always judicious and the answer was "yes." And that is the secret—I do not bother authorities about small things and all reasonable great requests are granted me. The man starts with his furlough tomorrow morning.

Sept. 12th, 1864. This is Monday morning. It is splendid here. Last night Anna Etheridge staid all night with me. She is of newspaper renown and is deserving I guess. Has staid with the third Michigan Regt. for more than three years. I have a very nice tent and keep a spare bed. There are two ladies riding on horseback this morning. I ought to be out but have no errand and do not often go in the day time unless I have to. For fear Sarah does not get her letters, I will say Dr. D. stopped to see Will on his way down, found him well and happy. I am perfectly well. If you could only know how I live here. Will thinks it is paradise almost, such a change from the breastworks. The Surg. here wants me to take charge of the low diet in the whole Div., but I won't do it—it is too much care. I want everything that I send home taken especial care of as I attach particular importance to everything before I take the trouble to send.

Sept. 10th, 1864.

MY DEAR SARAH

I RECEIVED thy letter last evening and had almost come to the conclusion that thee had forgotten me. There is nothing better than to get a good letter from home. There is no cause for anxiety for me. I am a person endowed with good sense. If I was sick for one day, would leave this land and be at home before three days. Some of the ladies remain here during a spell of sickness. It is terrible to be sick here for a lady. But there is no necessity of remaining, and *I*

148

should not after my usefulness was over. All the poetry was written by Albert Dod. Addie York's is quite a novelty. I am glad thee went to Salem. Eugene York I have lost track of entirely. I will send Dr. Dudley's picture, not that it looks a mite like him, though if it did I would not be so generous with it. I have an opportunity of seeing the original about every two weeks or so, so I care very little for the picture, but want it taken good care of. I have commenced sending them home because every one handles them here and they get soiled. James Bradway did not go to war and get killed. I suppose that is a melancholy satisfaction to his friends. I should hardly think it worth while for Rebecca to grieve much for a dead person for she certainly will be soon with them in heaven.

Mary sticks to the school well. Is any reason assigned to the public for Auxencico's ceasing his attentions in that direction? John Foley and Martha would be a good match to torment a sane brain. Martha must not visit our house while I am at home. I must have the floor then, and that *is* impossible when Martha is round. I still think I will come home some time in next month. Dr. Dudley will not be able to come with me. He will not get a leave of absence until they go into winter Qrs. unless he is sick, which I hope he will not be. Capt. Dod did not know particulars of Henry whatever. He has been heard from, however; is at Charleston prison, will meet lots of my friends there. Nellie Dudley wrote to her brother Fred an awful account of the treatment of our prisoners at Andersonville. I am not a believer in the awful accounts that have come from Libbey. Dr. Dudley was here to see me last night, stopped on his way to see William and found him first rate.

Copperheads I shall not listen to if I do come home, but a copperhead in the army is the most missplaced affair that ever was thought of. Jersey politics is a discredit to any people, but many Jersey people are estimable, I think, so I do not wish it sunk.

From thy attached aunt, CORNELIA HANCOCK
1st Div. 2nd Corps Hospt.

149

Sep. 16th, 1864.

MY DEAR SISTER

I WROTE to Dr. about receiving the $50 that Capt. Harris expressed for me. I received two pictures of Capt. Dod and a very nice letter from his mother. I received a letter from thee this evening dated Sep. 13, with the ruffle all in good order.

I hope Weatherlow has not forgotten me, for altho I have seen many soldiers since, I have not forgotten him. It seems funny to me to hear of anyone sitting down reading Tennyson's poems! It is all right, however. We have about as much as we can attend to, keeping the Rebs from gobbling us up. Last evening they took a herd of cattle and a lot of cavalry men right at our door. Today our rifle pits are manned and batteries planted within 1/4 mile of the hospital. I went on horse back a mile or so from camp and the infantry was moving in all directions. I do not feel concerned at all. I know I am as brave as half the people in this hospital and will stand my ground as well. I do not know what to make of those omnipresent rebs. But do hope sometime we will find them not vigilant. I miss my saddle very much. But the ladies round camp are very kind lending me. I know Emily Howland leaves Washington reluctantly. William's time is drawing to a close very fast. We are and have been expecting a big fight here, but it seems delayed from day to day. I received a very nice letter from Mother this evening. Take good care of the pictures. Give my love to Mr. Chapel. I do not know Col. Hepgood. That is no reason why he should not know me, however, for lots of soldiers know me whom I do not know. That sermon I enjoyed thee sent me last. It is sorrowful to reflect upon Mary Childs' situation. How does she bear it herself? How is the box directed? Always state that, also date of shipment. I have no doubt but it will come all right.

Elizabeth shall hear from the wine. I will send thee one picture of Capt. Dod. I have two. I cannot spare the best one. I do not know when I shall get home as there is a talk of consolidating the low diet kitchens in our Div. There are now three. The charge would be given to me and if I was away I should lose my chance. The Dr. in charge would give it to me without a question. He is a smart little Irish man who knows what is what. But the Surg. in charge of the Corps boards with Mrs. Holstein and for *personal* interest he does not want *her* establishment disturbed. So I do not know how they will make it. I would a little rather have a diet kitchen. I have always, then, a table for my friends. To be in the wards is not half the care. I shall not take it to heart anyway they choose to fix it. But will not lose my kitchen by being *away*.

I wish thee could see the meals that our soldiers get. They are *good*. When I think how we mussed at Gettysburg, the way I live now is paradise. I have four officers who board with me. We have just as nice meals as you do and nice dishes and have it waited on and much less confusion than at yours. I have excellent help now. I have discarded all my shirks. I have a man who was three years in the Continental. It is the most magnificent moonlight evenings. I have one friend in Camp, a Dr. Olmstead. He is a very handsome man. He is the only one who ever visits my quarters except on business. I do not give them any encouragement as a general thing. But Dr. Olmstead seems very gentlemanly and I get on with him very well so far. He accidentally shot himself in his foot while he and Dr. Dudley were fooling. It just passed over Dr. Dudley's head and thru the top of Olmstead's foot.

Sep. 17, 1864—There is nothing new to state, I believe, and will say I am perfectly well and happy and do not know at all when I can come home.   from thy sister, CORNELIA HANCOCK
I keep Eddie's flag to look at all the time.

Sept. 25th, 1864.

MY DEAR MOTHER

I AM waiting for the poking old Christian Com to fill an order for me and here is beautiful pen and ink handy so I write to say William is lying in my bed fast asleep and the Regt. relieved from the breastworks and out of danger: expects to go North on Tuesday

151

next. I shall go as soon as a hospital boat goes north. If I can get on board one I can go free of charge and it is much pleasanter to have something to do on a journey than to be entirely idle. We have men very sick in hospital now, they will be loathe to have me leave but I am afraid there will be a big battle here soon and I want to be *back* then. I received a letter from thee and Sallie and lots from all around, cannot complain of any one's attention to my wants. Last evening there was an illumination ordered in hospital for Sheridan's victories and the variety of devices upon the lanterns was quite wonderful considering the opportunity to get material.

I was presented with one for my quarters that took everything else down, a large ship painted, named the Gen. Hancock. I was, unfortunately, sick and could not go out that night but they would bring it in and light it for me. I was sick but one day and I might as well have been in an arcade for all the privacy that is possible for me. *Seven* doctors visited me in the course of the day, and every other functionary possible. The cause of my sickness was a late and very hearty supper. I am so recovered from my dyspepsia that when I do have a turn it seems as if I could bear it so much better. I thought while sick at my stomach how helpless I used to be and *now* how strong. I have gained here, better than any fortune, my nearly perfect health. A boon no one can appreciate until as long deprived as I have been.

I expect to start in a hospital transport tomorrow morning for some Northern port and shall be home sometime. Today is Sept. 25th, 1864.

CORNELIA HANCOCK

Back at City Point, Sunday, Oct. 17th, 1864.

MY DEAR SISTER

I ARRIVED at City Point perfectly safely, but had my passage to pay all the way from Baltimore here, which took all my money; it is an outrage, but the innocent always have to suffer for the

152

guilty. Thee had better send me the balance of the $10. after all my debts are paid. I found all frantic with joy to see me. They had been sending to the Point for me Wednesday and Thursday but had given up Friday. I got up, however, very comfortably as Tom and George were both watching for me.

The order has come for the consolidation of all the cook houses in our Div. and at present Mrs. Holstein has the charge. It is Burmeister's order and by every other Doctor and functionary disapproved. There will be a strong under current running her out of office. They are going tomorrow to build my log house for my winter qrts. I am perfectly satisfied. I have so many friends working for me I have nothing to do but let them alone. It will come out all right. Dr. O'Meagher says he would not go thru such another siege as he endured immediately after my departure for any money. Dr. Olmstead is well and was real glad to see me. Ribble is very much chagrined that I did not get the cookhouse. I tell him never fret. I have done nothing yet. The hosp. is quite empty. And they are building for winter Qrs. I rode up to the 12 N. J. Regt. and told the Jersey news. Dr. Dudley rode up along the breastworks and showed me into Petersburg. The men at the Regts. live in kind of underground huts. Shells were flying pretty lively. One man was killed while I was there. The weather is delightful here. The letters that were written from this hospt. were numerous. They did not half of them reach me.

I will write as things develope. Bridgett was very pleased with her saque. Her tent was a sight to see, all stowed with every thing belonging to me and looked laughable. Dr. Aiken arrived here today; looks as if he had better settle his accounts with the government and prepare for paradise.

from thy sister, CORNELIA HANCOCK

Oct. 29th, 1864, City Point.

MY DEAR SISTER

ANOTHER battle has been fought on the left with no particular re-

153

sults further than filling our hospital with poor, mangled human beings.

Dr. Dudley was on the field with his Regt. and is now a prisoner in the hands of the Rebels, if he is living.[1] Maj. Broadcut of his Regt. was brought in wounded and last evening said Dr. Dudley sent his horses to the rear and gave his new gold watch to Dr. Scott and went right out on to the field with the wounded. I suppose it is all right or it would not have been; only a few hours ago I got a note from him dated the 24th, saying they were packed up to leave and he hoped we would soon "meet in Richmond, *not* as prisoners of war." I have charge of the cookhouse and am just as busy as I can be anyway. I am well and very glad to be here in an active campaign. I do not feel much like writing; everything is suffering here now.

Write to me. Do not send me any money. I suppose Dr. Dudley's things will be sent to me and if I get into any trouble I can use his money. I wish he had some of his money with him, but I suppose the Johnnies would have taken it from him.

from thy sister, CORNELIA HANCOCK

I could not live here without working hard. My mind would not be contented and my mind is the principal part of me—I have very little physical. I am well almost all the time. Bridget does not live with me at present but does everything I want her to. Dr. Dudley may fare well, he may not. It is time he was heard from. I wish we could hear from Henry again. I have written to him. Lincoln is elected beyond a doubt, Grant's telegrams tell us. I think you have a part of the hardships of this rebellion to bear being separated most of the time from your children. I should think it would be hard when one is *blest with such children as you are*—ironical, of course.

I hope William will succeed in his Washington scheme, simply because he wishes it himself. If he knew Washington as well as I

[1] Surgeon Frederick A. Dudley, of the 14th Conn. Regiment, was left behind at Hatchers Run with medical supplies to take charge of the wounded who could not be moved. He was taken prisoner, was paroled Jan. 14th, 1865, but was not released to rejoin his regiment until after Lee's surrender in April.

154

do he would not want to live there. It is the most hellish place ever I tarried in. William has written to me. What is the matter with Waddington. Willie ought to write to me.

I would always be glad to receive a Salem paper. Remember me to poor Ruth, her race is nearly run. I do take care of myself. *Nov. 11, 11 o'clock, 1864*

from thy daughter, C. HANCOCK
1st Div. 2nd Corps.

City Point, Va., Nov. 14, 1864.

MY DEAR MOTHER

I THOUGHT I ought to have a letter from thee today but was disappointed.

With the abundance of time hanging upon thy hands thee ought to keep thy children well written to. I have had a cold for quite a while but am in hopes of recovering from it without absolutely taking my bed upon it. Dr. Aiken is in charge of our division now. How much I like him in that capacity I can hardly express. He is building a nice house for himself in view of having his sister down, and says if Ellen wishes to come he will lend it to me to entertain her in. I think it too long and exposing a journey to make in the dead of winter but if they choose to come I shall be very glad to see them. This is a splendid morning (Nov. 18th, 1864) everything is preparing for winter. Nothing is doing in the front. The officers from Dudley's regiment called to see me yesterday and not a word has been heard from him. There is one plausible supposition that he may be sent far south. If so he will be exchanged by the way of Port Royal in order to see his family. In any event every day that passes makes more uncertainty about him as he is not a man for want of energy to fail to write and would most probably write to me first, knowing I have intercourse with his Regt. and friends all in the army. He has now been a prisoner for 22 days. The surgs. at Reams Station fight were exchanged almost immediately.

155

Nov. 23rd—I believe I received a short letter from thee a few days ago. This one has remained unfinished quite a while. I have 350 patients now on light diet and any one may know that is considerable care. There is very little doing in the military world. The sick were sent to the rear, 8 days' rations issued, men called out with knapsacks, packed tents, all jerked up, and God sent a driving storm upon us and no move could be made nor comfort had for the men. I wrote to Ellen and Sallie yesterday. Dr. Olmstead goes to the front tomorrow. There is a constant change going forward all the while here. How well Sarah seems to be getting along. I guess we have been lucky in the selection of a school. There seems a more healthy atmosphere to pervade the school than is common in the generality of boarding schools. Send me some pieces of poetry out of the newspapers. Dr. Burmeister, our former Surg. in charge of the Corps, has been removed and a Dr. Parker from Camp Parole, Annapolis, takes his place. The hospital demanded a change and I am very thankful it has been made.

Write to me. I have not heard one word from Fred [Dr. Dudley].

from thy daughter, C. HANCOCK

My love to father

. . . Capt. Dubois it is thought will be major. Chew, the Regt. desire, should be made Col. He is a deserving man and well liked in the Regt. I have supposed father was knitting when I did not picture him asleep. I am not surprised to hear they are buying a boat.

I am glad Oxy came out in a speech; would much like to see it. Jersey is gone up for any hope of reformation. Dr. Ribble, a particular friend of mine, because he came from Jersey, is the most flagrant democrat. He seems sound about most other topics but insists upon that; all the people near where he lives (Belvidere) are democrats, so he is too. There seems to be something in the soil of North Jersey productive of human copperheads.

I am sorry to hear that Quinton and Mary have to lose their baby. I believe I did not know they had a baby. It makes me think of Susie Irelan's remark when Rosa Pierce's baby was dying:

156

"Them that has, has to lose them; them that han't can't." Our family seems prosperous. My prayer is it may continue so while there is a war and after its close; a few domestic troubles would seem but trifles to me. Give my love to Rebecca. I am afraid I shall get home in time to go to her funeral yet.

I wonder the "Aid" in Salem has held together as long as it has, composed of so many incongruious elements. The people of this world have one thing to learn, that if perfectly learned would be of immense service to each and every one—"To live and to let live." I have no doubt Lydia White is doing a great deal of good. She is in just such a hospt as I am, belonging I suppose now to the 24th Army Corps in the Army of the James. After it comes to be pleasant and warm weather I will ride over to see her. It is only about five miles from here. I have not left the bounds of this hospt. since the 15th day of October but you must remember this *hospital* is larger than Hancock's Bridge and vastly more populous.

I hope to hear from Sallie soon. I don't know why Lydia White should need supplies in a base hospt like here. Here I do think we have as near everything for the comfort of the sick as it is possible to get into the army. There is a great difference I know about the efficiency of the Surg-in-charge and she may have a poor one. I have in my kitchen three elegant large cooking stoves, a zinc baking oven 6 feet by three, one caldron holding 60 gallons and two 20 each, feed mostly under three hundred men. The hospital department has improved beyond any other branch of the service. Our sick are now brought from the extreme front in Hospital cars which are beds suspended upon elastic bands so there is very little jarring.

Ellen's box arrived, both cakes with scarcely a crumb of the icing broken. I had no concern about the boxes until they were set down in the kitchen. The men opened them and exclaimed at the beauty of the cakes. I hope father is quite well. I am very anxious for all my relatives to remain alive until the war is over. I shall enjoy my home so much I know. There is some prospect of my

157

being paid $16. a month. If it is offered I shall not refuse it. That amount would make me very independent the way I now live. This is Sunday, a beautiful, cold winter day. The Bible says: "Cleanliness is next to Godliness." We are next to Godly here today, then, for everything is as clean as possible. Dr. Dalton, Medical Director of this post, was thru my quarters today and paid me this compliment: "If any one in this Army was deserving good quarters it was Miss Hancock."

from thy daughter, CORNELIA HANCOCK

Nov. 28th, 1864. City Point, Va.

MY DEAR SISTER

TODAY is Monday, a beautiful cheerful looking morning. Butler's guns are pounding away and were yesterday. Thanksgiving day is passed. We received here forty turkeys as our share of the donation from the North. It was a small ration for so many men but they seemed to be pleased with what they got. I think there was a great proportion of the beneficence went to the front, I hope so. At Christmas we hope to give our hospital a good treat. It is wonderful in what a good state of preservation the turkeys were that came all the way from N. York. The boat was grounded and did not arrive until the day following Thanksgiving, but that was a small matter. A new cook-house is being built and if I have the charge of it shall have spacious quarters to entertain my friends in. Miss Hart has gone North this morning, will call to see thee and she will give a glowing description of me. She is one of my particular friends among the ladies. Dr. Dudley has never been heard from. I hope he will be back by Christmas.

Dr. Olmstead has been made Surgeon of his Regiment, but has not been relieved from here yet, but expects to leave every day. Dr. Aiken still remains in charge of our division. How dreadfully he coughs but we get along first rate.

The men are really at work with a vigor (for soldiers) getting their Barracks along today.

158

I believe I told thee Dr. Burmeister had been relieved and a Dr. Parker from Annapolis put in his place. Burmeister was a nice man but not master of his position by any means.

Nov. 29th, 1864.

Miss Hart gave me a pair of Andirons and I must tell of it. I enjoy them so much. Before I had to sit up nights to keep my fire from rolling out and burning my house down. The new kitchen is 72 ft. by 20, so you may know something of its dimensions. I want a corset lacer sent in the next letter. I want, if thee wants to spend any money for me at Christmas, to get some of my photographs. It seems impossible to get along here without giving some of mine away. I would like three of each copy of mine got and sent to me by Christmas. And if any of your circle of friends intend doing anything for soldiers at Christmas let them send their outpourings to me. I should not wonder if we attempt to set a nice table for the hospital then and I would like to receive some boxes of cakes for the occasion. I expect some from N. Y. Do not forget Dr. Olmstead's tobacco bag. He left this morning to go to his Regiment and it is on the advance picket-line, where the firing is incessant. Says he intends to volunteer to remain behind with the wounded in the next fight if there is anyone called upon. He will then try to hunt Fred up. But will not find him, of course. Doctor is bad off somewhere or we should have heard from him before this. Does any one hear from Henry? When the cold weather sets in will it not be awful for them? We sent our sick to Washington this morning. A big fight is expected. I dread it very much. Butler's guns are pounding away most furiously this morning. If thee was here thee would be sure thy last hour had come.

How does John prosper in his occupation. How is Edward. Little Tom's picture is very much admired. Too bad Fred did not get his to take to Richmond. (I mean the one thee took so much pains with).

I have not received a letter from thee in a long while.

from thy sister, C. HANCOCK

159

Nov. 30th, 1864.

MY DEAR MOTHER

IT seems quite a while since I have heard from thee. That is hardly an excuse for not writing to thee, however. Maj. Chew came down from the Regiment and took dinner with me yesterday.

Dec. 1st, 1864. A most beautiful morning, much building going forward in the hospital. The new kitchen is to be 72 by 20 ft. long. My quarters in one end 20 by 18 ft. Is not that large enough to keep my little body comfortable in. Do not put any directions on my letters but 1st Div. 2nd Corps Hospital, City Point, Va.

Dec. 2nd. Still I receive no letters from home. I think it strange but all right, I suppose. I have long since made up my mind that all that happens is all right or I should not be near as happy as I am. Building is the order of the day here and cannonading up at the front.

Dec. 3rd. I wish you could have heard Butler's guns last night. It seemed as if thunderbolts from heaven were running riot in the land. I do not know the result. I received a short note from Ellen informing me that Willie had been quite sick, but no letter from thee or Sallie. Nothing happens here new or strange to tell. If you intend doing anything for the Christmas of soldiers, let your things be sent to me. No letter from thee tonight, Dec. 3rd.

Dec. 4th. A beautiful Sabbath morning. My kitchen is ready for inspection, a sight to see. I am going to have three turkeys for dinner. I have to attend to the officers' mess table now and the turkeys were bought for them. If thee was here thee could have a very good dinner. We have changed Surgeons-in-charge and a great improvement made. Inspection is over and all got good praise.

We have some very sick men here now but few wounded. If I could only hear from my Doctor I should be much more happy than I now am. Nothing has ever been heard from him. I see they are exchanging prisoners very rapidly from Southern prisons. I do not believe he went farther south than Libby. What was heard last from Henry? I have hope that Fred will be put upon duty

160

in some hospital. They will soon find he is a good operator. If so, he will fare well. If that had been the case I think tho he would have had a chance to have written before this. Nothing but conjecture can fill our minds, however; nothing definite is known except he was left upon the field at 10 o'clock at night in charge of our wounded. Dr. Olmstead, a great friend of mine, has been promoted and ordered to his Regt. so he is gone away now almost a week. Dr. Aiken is still in charge of our Division and we get along splendidly together. He is very sick, tho, most of the time, consumption. from thy daughter, C. HANCOCK

City Point, Va., Dec. 15th, 1864.

MY DEAR MOTHER

THY letter has at length come to hand but was not directed to the hospital and was advertised at City Point. If it had been directed *Miss* Hancock it would have come to me, but *Cornelia* Hancock does not seem to mean *me* out here. They supposed it to be some contraband at the Point.

I am well and full of business. My new kitchen is nearly finished. I shall move probably by Sunday. I shall then have to leave my log hut for more commodious quarters in my kitchen. I received a letter from Dr. Dudley's mother; she thinks he is dead. I shall never think so, if he never comes back. In fact, I have seen so many that were with him and they all say it is impossible that he can be dead. I honestly do not worry myself much about it. I know whatever is right will take place. I would like to hear the particulars of Henry's imprisonment. I am glad he is out. Fred's Billy (colored) stays with me now, blacks my shoes and takes care of Dr. Aiken and myself generally. Until this last letter I never knew what was the matter with father. I suppose Will had a good time at Cape May. I would like to have some quails but I get excellent living. If you can *live* I don't care anything about *taxes*. So you do not starve, and have a good house and have only one child in

161

the army and she not exposed to shot and shell, you ought to be very thankful. The poetry was beautiful. Sallie certainly is crazy not writing to thee. She writes to me quite frequently.

I am well, hope this will find you so. Send me that letter of Doctor Dudley's that is laying round your house somewhere I hope. I want it.

from thy daughter, CORNELIA

Give my love to father. I shall be home at shad-time.

City Point, Dec. 17th, 1864.

MY DEAR SISTER

How much I would like to see Henry. Tell me how he likes Seceshes. I hate them very badly indeed. Our Band is playing splendid music. Everything is going along after the same old fashion here. Miss Hart I expected back today but was disappointed. I suppose a few days will bring her. I am sorry to have you use your own money to send the Christmas box for we will not need the things as badly as that. I shall be glad to make some contributions to the table but any one as poor as I am ought not to make a show. How did I come by the snow shoes? I hope they have some warmth in them. I suffer so much with the cold in my feet. William wrote me to know if I could get him a pass to come to see me. I sent him a letter to Genl. Ashley and if that does not succeed I can get him a pass from here and send him. I heard today, but I do not know when he wants to come, now, or in the winter. He did not tell me where to direct nor anything about it, or how long he intended remaining in Washington.

Did Steward Fox call to see you? There will be a constant stream of persons coming from here on leaves of absence as the winter advances. I suppose you would like to see them so I shall send them along.

Today is Sunday, the only day we know in the seven because it is inspection. Next week will be a busy week, moving into the kitchen and the week after Christmas I suppose I shall have my

162

hands full as usual. I got a very good letter from Mrs. Dod last evening. She regrets very much she did not know when I was North. She says she would have left anything to have come to see me. If ever the war is over I shall visit her. I get very interesting letters from Miss Rebecca and S. A. Ingham, but from no one else in Salem. I have another deserter in my wards. My last one died the day before his pardon came. This one, I think, will die too. The mind has such an effect upon the body, we cannot get them to rally a mite. Dr. Aiken takes charge of the sick of my section, so I have a very satisfactory time with them. He seems better and takes stimulants enough to bring him to life even if he were dead altogether. Dr. Parker, our present Surg-in-charge, is first rate, such an improvement upon Burmeister. Cannonading is constant here almost, and nothing comes of it that I hear. We hope Savannah is taken. from thy sister, C. HANCOCK

City Point, Dec. 29th, 1864.

MY DEAR SISTER

CHRISTMAS is over. We had it to perfection here, a splendid dinner for 1400 men; just to think of it, cooking a sumptuous dinner of turkeys, pies, etc. for that number. Is it not appalling? Miss Hart had charge of the dinner and, of course, it was a success. She is so smart. I had moved into my new kitchen and gave her full sway there. It was handy to where the dinner was set in the government kitchen where 400 can be seated at once. The hall was decorated tastefully with evergreens and was really pretty as a picture. It was photographed, I believe. I have a splendid kitchen and no mistake, a large dining room, and a nice room to live in. I occupy the most prominent position in the hospital, have a great deal of care, but not much real work to do. I was in hopes Miss Hart would get the other kitchen but it was decided to give it to Mrs. Sampson, a very slow individual. However, I am satisfied; Miss Hart now gets her meals for her sick and herself at my kitchen and we get along first rate. A flag of truce has been sent over to the Rebs. with an inquiry as to the situation or fate of Dr. Dudley & company. It has not been heard from yet. Much solicitation is felt by the officers of his Brigade since such a long time has elapsed and nothing heard. It is very complimentary that such an inquiry be made. I never heard of the like being done before. Billy (Dudley's col'd boy) stays with me yet.

Dec. 30th, 1864. It is a beautiful cold morning. Dr. Olmstead has been down once to see me since he went to his Regiment. Bridgett washes my clothes. She quarrels with the men too much to be in a winter kitchen. I see that she is made comfortable and has everything she needs.

I am this moment talking to the most silly kind of a Christian. He wishes to know if I have *experienced Religion?* Will wrote me quite a description of Henry's adventures. Has he a leave of absence or is he discharged? I should think he had *done* soldiering now. I have just had notice that a New Years dinner is to be prepared. So good-bye to writing any more.

from thy sister, CORNELIA HANCOCK

City Point, Va., Jan. 6th, 1865.

MY DEAR MOTHER

I RECEIVED thy letter dated Jan. 2nd this evening. Was pleased to hear you were getting along well. I shall never receive those back letters so write whenever thee feels like it.

I have had a full description of Henry through Isabella who exceeds all my correspondents in descriptive powers. I would like to see Henry. William says he is at his old occupation, quarrelling with cousin Bell.

Dr. Dudley has not been heard from. I shall never think he is dead. I hope soon to hear from him. It is infamous to hold a noncombatant when he was left behind in the hands of the rebels as an act of humanity. I am sure, however, that he will get back safe again.

Sallie Harris can have the pleasing intelligence that the box has arrived in the most perfect order, not in time for Christmas but a few days since. The things were much more highly appreciated than if received at Christmas for we had so many luxuries then. The mince pies I took into a ward where there were 17 wounded men all doing well. I gave them each a piece of pie and they gave three cheers for Jersey. There is not a class of persons in the world more cheerful than a ward full of wounded who are doing well.

I will write to Dr. Satterthwait to indorse strongly a furlough for Elisha Stewart. He ought to have it, and be honored in Alloways Creek as a soldier who has never been to the rear in this arduous campaign. You must have more snow than we. A very little has fallen here. I received the Standard with the notice of Mrs. Farnham. I would like to see Beulah's children very much. I do not believe their mother will allow them to forget me. I have become so used to being here that it seems like home to me. I am moved entirely into the new kitchen. I am never exposed now at all. My fire is made before I get out of bed, I have beautiful private quarters; everything nice to cook with in my kitchen. If you could only spend a day here and see my operations it would add much to my happiness. . . .

Our last battle I believe to be a perfect failure. The Rebels did a sharp trick the other night, just dressed up in *our* uniforms and marched round in our rear, and relieved our pickets one by one until they captured about 200 of our men. The night was extremely dark. The devil or some smart person seems to help them. I am very tired of them indeed.

from thy daughter, CORNELIA HANCOCK
Give my love to father. I should think thee would be very lonesome.

March 3rd, 1865.

MY DEAR SISTER

I WRITE to say Billy brought the things through, all very safely. I wear the skirt for a dress, it is much admired as well as the hood.

165

The hood had almost better have been a hat. The other things were all nice and acceptable. I have the kindest friends of any among the ladies here. They all have to toil dreadfully to get along with their clothes. Dr. G. T. Ribble has his leave and starts from here on Sunday morning, March 5th. After that and before 15 days are out he will call to see thee. Anne Etheridge is now ordered from the front to stay at the hospt. and is very bare of clothes. She wants thee to buy her a skirt exactly like mine and two pairs of stockings like my old brown ones. If there are any of my white stockings that I did not bring with me send them. My blue gingham dress I want, and what will add more to my comfort than anything else would be to send me a pair of corsets. Mine are all to pieces and when warm weather comes I shall need them much. Find just what Anne's things cost and I will give Dr. Child $10. of her money to pay thee. I feel that if this hospt. stays just as it is I shall not come home before the 12 N. J.'s time is out which will be in Sept. next, for I hate to travel and have no money to do it with. If I can get decent clothes to stay here with I will be content. I thought of sending Anne's money in this letter, but thought it might get lost. Dr. will give it to thee. The Black thread is the length of half the bosom of my corset, the white thread half the waist. I always have bought mine in Arch below fifth.

Col. Baxter is making some improvement in the knapsack. He does not think but that it will be possible for him to get it introduced. When I read about Mrs. Holstein to the boys in the kitchen they all laughed. Mrs. Lee wishes to return to the army, but none are allowed at the front and Dr. Parker will allow no more here, so I guess she will not get here except probably for a visit. Mrs. Lee is one of the *best* friends a soldier ever had. Try to make Dr.'s bundle as small as possible.

from thy sister, NELLIE HANCOCK

Give my love to Willie. I expect to answer his letter.

March 7th, 1865.

MY DEAR MOTHER

IT seems to me quite a while since I received any letter from thee but always take it for granted no news is good news. The weather is most beautiful here. I think it has been the most beautiful winter I ever spent anywhere. Dr. Ribble, one of our officers, left here on a Leave of Absence. He will call to see Ellen. He is a very good friend of mine. I do not know that I will come home this spring. I want to be home when the 12 N. J.'s time is out and that is in Sept. and it will not pay to go home twice in so short a time. And, too, I have no money. It costs me nothing to stay here. Time passes every day. I am contented while I know you are all well. What more does a person want in this world. This weather lasts and a *move* must come in this army. Then our hospital work will be so active that I shall not have time to go home.

March 8th. Time passes very rapidly here. It is raining in the most persevering manner. But it does not affect me any. My house is tight and I have very few errands out.

from thy daughter, CORNELIA H.

167

IX

RICHMOND TAKEN

❖

April 1st, 1865.

MY DEAR MOTHER

I RECEIVED thy letter by Elisha. He called on his way to his Regt. Seemed to have had a pleasant visit at home. He was right about my manner of living. It is more than comfortable.

He just missed one fight. I have not heard from him since the very last fight. We expect 400 wounded down tonight. You did not say anything about Sullivan's School in your last letter. Did Mary Ann get it? Ellen writes to me very faithfully. Sallie's poetry was very good. I feel almost sure I shall not be home until Sept. as business will be brisk here. Time passes and we hardly know how it goes.

April 3rd. This morning we could see the flames of Petersburg lighting the skies. About 5 miles of our line have opened fire and no one can sleep. We can see flashes from the firing and there is a deafening roar. The question in all our minds is: "Will the Rebels take breakfast with us or we with them?"

I suppose the Rebels are compelled to evacuate the place. Our troops can enter now at any time. Sheridan occupies the S. Side road, our Corps supports him, &c. All news is cheering this morning. . . .

A telegram was received here that Gen. Weitzel entered *Richmond* this morning at 8 A.M. There is great rejoicing here, of course. The wounded are constantly coming in. Day after tomorrow I am invited to go to Richmond on one of the first boats. If we get the wounded tolerably comfortable, I shall go and get a

168

relick of old Libby and take my dinner at the Spotswood House. I can give no information of the fate of any of my friends, and that is one great reason we withhold our great rejoicing to see how many are left to rejoice with us. I have just come in from the train but none that I know have yet come in. I write you I am well, shall probably be one of the first Union women in Richmond, and on no account have any concern for me. I shall get along all right. We are ordered to be ready to move at a moment's notice and in every way we are liable to change. I shall write as often as I can but if I don't you may know that I am busy is the reason I do not.

from thy daughter, CORNELIA HANCOCK
2nd Corps D. F. Hospt., City Point, Va.

April 11th, 1865.

MY DEAR SISTER

R ICHMOND *is taken.* I visited the city April 9th and saw for myself that Gen. Weitzel has his headquarters in Jeff's mansion; perfect order prevails in the town. On that day the patients had been removed to Washington so as to have plenty of room for the wounded when Lee would surrender. So, as there was comparatively little to be done, we took horses on a steamboat that was going to Richmond to carry supplies for the soldiers guarding Richmond, and rode through the city. The lower part of the city was smouldering with a fire started by the Rebels before leaving. The white people were all hidden away in their houses, but the colored people were jubilant and on the streets in gay attire. We visited Libby Prison that was at this time filled with Rebel prisoners. Flowers were blooming and the weather was mild. Beauty was apparent even in the desolate, dejected city. We saw Jeff Davis' head quarters, but no Jeff Davis there.

Lee has now surrendered. We were wholly unconscious of it until we returned to City Point, when the great rejoicing at General

Grant's headquarters proclaimed the fact. The salutes were fired here yesterday at noon. A bloodless surrender keeps our hospital still empty and we have time to give special attention to a few who are dying just when they want most to live. After nightfall, I walk up and down my long, deserted stockade, I see the great change from war to no war, and brace myself for a new order of things.

President Lincoln visited our hospital a few days since. When the medical directors wanted to call his attention to the appointments of the hospital, he said: "Gentlemen, you know better than I *how* to *conduct* these hospitals, but I came here to take by the hand the men who have achieved our glorious victories." After that the men who were able stood in line and he shook hands with them—and the others, he went to their bedsides and spoke to *them*. He assured us the war would be over in six weeks. I shall come home when the 12th N. Jersey is mustered out of service, let that be sooner or later. Before we heard of Lee's surrender I boxed up all my winter clothing thinking we should move. There are two good sized boxes now on their way directed to Doctor. You will have to pay the express bill at your end of the line as they will not receive pay here. One of the boxes belongs to Anne Etheridge, the other is mine. Mine had better be opened as my best dress will be well jambed. Do not disturb any of my papers nor little traps, for they are all very valuable to me if they do not look so to you.

The prisoners are passing here all the while. Gen. Ewell passed here last evening. Most of our wounded have been brought to City Point and I do not know what our army is at. Col. More of 14th Conn. Vol. is here wounded. Gen. Smyth, command of our Brig., was killed; you will see his picture among my others. Dr. Ribble and Olmstead are both at the front now and I hear very little from them. No communication by mail. Dudley is all right so far. I am well and very busy finishing up this Rebellion. I hope we shall get thru before the heat of summer. I have not had a letter in quite a while. My gingham dress I shall never get made. I would like to have the other one sent as soon as possible.

from thy sister, NELLIE HANCOCK
2nd Corps D. F. Hospt., City Point, Va.

May 3rd, 1865.

MY DEAR SISTER

Do not send any of the various articles until thee hears from me again as I am liable to be at home any day and may not be at home for a month, but in either case I shall not need my dress as I have the other one made and it looks very nicely. Dr. Ribble came down from his Regiment last evening with the last lot of sick I hope ever to see come to our hospt. They were not very sick, only could not march to Washington to which place, after they rendezvous at Manchester opposite Richmond, they are ordered to go. The men, of course, are in exuberant spirits which is very refreshing to see after the many toilsome days they have spent. Do not fail to write me and direct the same. I cannot leave here until this hospt is done and no one can say how long that will be. I hope thee will soon be better and I will soon be home; the days seem long to me now.

from thy sister, NELLIE

2nd Corps D. F. Hospt., May 13th, 1865.
Near Alexandria

MY DEAR SISTER

I SUPPOSE thee is in N. J. attending the Anti Slavery meeting, as I see by the papers it is in session. The last thing, on board the boat leaving City Point I received a letter from thee. We left the Point May 10th, arrived in Alexandria May 12th, and came out into a beautiful field to establish a resting place for the tired and sick of the Corps when it arrives. The situation is splendid, the air so fresh

171

and altogether it seems like getting out of prison to get away from City Point, we were there so long.

Dr. Aiken did not come with us here. Dr. Vansant, an entirely new doctor, takes charge. He picked me out of the eight on duty to accompany this hospt to this place. I was very sick on the voyage but feel all the better for that now. I have never spent a more pleasant day, have my kitchen all started, am now sitting outdoors with the same family lying round a splendid camp fire. The Whip-poor-wills are singing as I thought they never sung except at William's. I would like to be home but shall enjoy seeing the Corps come up and see all my friends, some of whom I have not seen since Lee surrendered. What a joyful party will come up either today or tomorrow.

We have no sick here at all but soon will have. I have no women with me at all. Mike and the rest of my family all with me. I like Dr. Vansant well. His family lives in Alexandria and we shall not see much of him. Dr. Aiken will come up soon. Dr. Ribble came to Washington the day before I did and I do not know where he is now, suppose loafing round Washington. Dr. Dudley again has charge of the 2nd Div. hospt. and will soon be here. Just to think of all the people I know whom I will see in the next few days. "Muster out" is on every soldier's brain at present.

Some of the soldiers from the Corps are straggling along up to my camp fire. I have just ordered them some supper and they are very talkative.

If there is a prospect of the Corps staying here for a month or so I shall come home and make a visit and return. If this (as we think it will be) is temporary I shall finish up before I come home for good. I shall *not go to Mexico*. Sunday morning the paper boys came along crying the news: "Jeff Davis captured in women's clothes. Jeff Davis captured in women's clothes." 1

from thy sister, NELLIE HANCOCK

1 Jefferson Davis, President of the Confederacy, was captured May 10th.

172

. . . On the first day's review in Washington I saw the Army of the Potomac from the piazza of a country house where I could speak to those I knew. When Sherman's army passed I was on the President's Grand Stand and saw General Sherman as he passed from the Treasury Building to the White House—the only moving figure—he was mounted on a fine black horse, with all the bands playing: "Hail to the Chief, the conquering hero comes." That very afternoon I returned to Philadelphia.

from thy daughter, CORNELIA H.